# Music Librarianship at the Turn of the Century

### Richard Griscom
editor

### Amanda Maple
assistant editor

*Music Library Association*
*Technical Reports, No. 27*

The Scarecrow Press, Inc.
Lanham, Maryland, and London
2000

# SCARECROW PRESS, INC.

Published in the United States of America
by Scarecrow Press, Inc.
4720 Boston Way, Lanham, Maryland 20706
www.scarecrowpress.com

4 Pleydell Gardens, Folkestone
Kent CT20 2DN, England

British Library Cataloguing-in-Publication Information Available

**Library of Congress Cataloging-in-Publication Data**

Music librarianship at the turn of the century / edited by Richard Griscom and Amanda Maple.
     p. cm. — (MLA technical reports ; no. 27)
    Includes bibliographical references and index.
    ISBN 0-8108-3866-4 (paper : alk. paper)
    1. Music librarianship. I. Griscom, Richard. II. Maple, Amanda, 1956– III. Series.
ML111 .M756 2000
026'.78—dc21                                         00-032949

# CONTENTS

———————— ◇ ————————

# FOREWORD

◇

So here we are, engulfed in a millennial madness utterly unrelated to anything performed by the earth and moon in all their
natural rotations and revolutions.

—Steven J. Gould[1]

The idea for this set of essays[2] came out of an afternoon trip to the corner coffeeshop, a busy campus meeting place that is distinct in nature and appearance from the brick-faced structures around it. The building was once home to an Italian restaurant, and I suspect the owners deco-rated it to resemble a Tuscan country house. Swirls of cream-colored stucco cover the exterior, and small panels of bas-relief sculpture are set over some of the doors and windows. The stucco continues inside, with dark brown beams extending across the ceiling and worn brown tiles covering the floor.

Faculty and students from the School of Music and the neighboring Chemical and Life Sciences Building can be found in the shop at all hours of the day and well into the evening. Although the coffee is good, it probably has little to do with the attraction of the place: the cof-feeshop offers a haven from university life—even if it happens to be filled with university folk. People go there to get away. When faculty and students take the short walk down the street to the shop, they leave be-hind their offices, classrooms, and practice rooms and enter neutral territory. They might find themselves talking about what they had just left behind, but a change in scene can offer a change in perspective. Sometimes words that could not be spoken in the offices can be said here, and thoughts that were suppressed in the red-brick buildings can be released here. A trip around the corner can be a simple break from routine; occasionally, it is a time of discovery and epiphany.

On this particular December afternoon in 1998, I was walking to the coffeeshop with a friend from the musicology department—someone who also edited a journal. In our occasional trips for coffee, we would each lend a sympathetic ear to the other's latest editorial trials. (Often conversation centered on articles: his complaint was having too many;

---

1. Stephen J. Gould, *Questioning the Millennium: A Rationalist's Guide to a Precisely Arbitrary Countdown* (New York: Harmony Books, 1997), 22.
2. Originally published in *Notes: Quarterly Journal of the Music Library Association* 56 (2000): 563–664.

1

mine, too few.) It was cold out, and snow filled the terra cotta planters on the wall separating the coffeeshop's patio from the sidewalk. All that remained of the annuals that had spilled over the sides of the boxes a few months ago were clumps of brown, shriveled stalks, looking like leafless miniature trees on a field of white.

We crossed the patio, entered the coffeeshop, and bought our drinks. After sitting down at a small round table and taking a few exploratory sips from our cups, conversation turned as usual to the journals.

"Are you planning to do anything for the millennium?" my friend asked.

"Do you mean a special issue?"

"Well, yes, that would be one way, I suppose."

"I've thought about it, but I'm not sure I want to fuel the frenzy. After all, it's just another year."

My friend cocked his head to one side and said, "Well, I wouldn't be able to do anything even if I wanted to. I have articles scheduled well into 2001. If it's possible for you, you might want to give it some thought. There's nothing necessarily bad about the idea."

We talked a bit longer and left. On subsequent solo trips to the coffeeshop, I did give the idea some thought.

I had been finding it difficult to know what to make of the passage into the new century. Despite all the best-of-the-century lists and multipart television retrospectives and advertisements for one-thousand-dollar-a-ticket New Year's Eve events, it was easy to look around and conclude that the transition to the next century held little of true significance to anyone's life. But regardless of my own doubts, millennial madness was marching onward, and I needed to decide whether to drag NOTES onto the bandwagon.

My first thought had been to play the cool sophisticate and nudge NOTES past the gaudy show without allowing it to turn its head. But as I sat in the coffeeshop and thought, I came around to the idea that the passing of the century could be an opportunity for members of our profession to take a trip of their own around the corner to reflect on where we are and offer insights into where we might be going. Past editors of NOTES have made a point of promoting such occasional musings,[3] and the published papers of watershed conferences have served the same

---

3. NOTES has published many articles that assess the state of various aspects of our profession and look ahead to the future; the two most recent general accounts are Ruth Watanabe, "American Music Libraries and Music Librarianship: An Overview in the Eighties," *Notes* 38 (1981): 239–56, and Mary Davidson, "American Music Libraries and Librarianship: Challenges for the Nineties," *Notes* 50 (1993): 13–22.

purpose.[4] Thoughtful essays on the state of our profession can help us gain perspective on the recent past as we prepare for the future.

As we round off one arbitrary block of one hundred years and enter another,[5] MLA also prepares to celebrate its seventieth anniversary, in 2001. What better time to pause for reflection? This is our moment, our own *fin de siècle*, a good time to stand up straight and take our measure.

\*     \*     \*

> We all need to orient ourselves in time, even if that means that we must use the clumsy labels of years and decades. The lack of any historical memory (even a false one) is like an attack of amnesia at the personal level. It deprives one of an identity. Though we do not learn to predict the future from the past, the greater our understanding of long stretches of time, the better become our chances of judging the past we all share in a convincing way.
>
> —Garry Wills[6]

In this issue, thirteen authors take that figurative trip around the corner to ponder the recent past, the present, and the near future as they affect various aspects of our profession. The essayists were given free rein in their approach to the topics. I did not define specific parameters for each essay, nor did I encourage the authors to contact each other to lay claim to certain borderline topics. As a result, some of the essays overlap, but I have let redundancies stand. Sometimes the different treatments represent different points of view; when they do not, the simple repetition of an issue reinforces its importance.

I asked the essayists to review the current state of affairs in their respective areas (prefaced by historical background if needed), to describe the challenges and concerns of the present, and to predict what we might expect to see during the next few years.[7] The essays are a chronicle of

---

4. For example, the proceedings of the 1986 conference on music bibliography (Richard Green, ed., *Foundations of Music Bibliography* [New York: Haworth Press, 1993]) and the papers of the 1989 Harvard symposium (Michael Ochs, ed., *Music Librarianship in America* [Cambridge: Eda Kuhn Loeb Music Library, Harvard University, 1991]).

5. Does the twenty-first century start in 2000 or 2001? Take your pick. I find myself more in sympathy with the Dionysian glee over the temporal odometer rolling over to 2000 than with the irrefutable Apollonian stance that the twenty-first century must begin with the year 2001 since the first century began with the year 1. Both years have their supporters. I first encountered an argument for 2001, simply expressed, in an unexpected place: Al Franken, *Rush Limbaugh Is a Big Fat Idiot and Other Observations* (New York: Island Books, 1996), 258. Stephen J. Gould, on the other hand, made it clear he would be donning his millennial party hat on 31 December 1999 in *Questioning the Millennium*, 112–13.

6. Garry Wills, "A Reader's Guide to the Century," *New York Review of Books,* 15 July 1999, 28.

7. Yes, predictions rarely come true and cannot be relied on for planning, but often our thoughts on what we expect to happen say as much about us and the age we live in as our observations on the past and present.

our profession's many accomplishments, occasional near misses, and rare failures; it is a story of professional cooperation and individual commitment.

So read on, and by reading, discover who we are and what we are thinking at this chance moment, we music librarians at the end of the twentieth century.

Richard Griscom
Editor, NOTES, 1997–2000

# COLLECTION DEVELOPMENT
# AND MANAGEMENT

## By Daniel Zager

—◇—

> Looking through the literature of music librarianship, one is
> struck by the curious fact that what is considered by music li-
> brarians to be their most profound and sacred professional
> trust—the intellectual activity of selecting materials with which
> to build strong collections—has received relatively little atten-
> tion.[1]

So wrote James B. Coover in 1973. Two aspects of this quotation de-
serve comment. First, more than twenty-five years later, one is struck by
the continuing dearth of literature dealing specifically with collection
development in music libraries.[2] Second, Coover's characterization of
collection development as a "profound and sacred professional trust" is a
concept that will not necessarily garner universal assent in the American
library world at the turn of the millennium.[3]

Less in academic music libraries than in the larger library systems of
which they are often a part, collection development as a discrete library
function has with some frequency of late been downgraded, the role of
bibliographers and subject specialists—who have the responsibility to

---

Daniel Zager is music librarian and adjunct associate professor of music at the University of North
Carolina at Chapel Hill.

1. James B. Coover, "Selection Policies for a University Music Library," in *Reader in Music Librarianship*,
ed. Carol June Bradley (Washington, D.C.: Microcard Editions Books, 1973), 236.
2. For example, under "collection development" and related terms in Karen R. Little, comp., *Notes: An
Index to Volumes 1–50* (Canton, Mass.: Music Library Association, 1995), one finds only a few articles related to collection development, management, and assessment, among them: K. Linda Ward, "Collection
Policy in College and University Libraries," *Notes* 29 (1973): 432–40, and Joan Kunselman, Peggy Daub,
and Marion Taylor, "Toward Describing and Assessing the National Music Collection," *Notes* 43 (1986):
7–13. Mary Wallace Davidson includes some cogent comments on collection development in her essay
"American Music Libraries and Librarianship: Challenges for the Nineties," *Notes* 50 (1993): 13–22. With
no intention here of being exhaustive, in sources other than *Notes* there is Michael A. Keller's chapter on
music in *Selection of Library Materials in the Humanities, Social Sciences, and Sciences*, ed. Patricia A. McClung
(Chicago: American Library Association, 1985): 139–63, and Edward Lein, "Suggestions for Formulating
Collection Development Policy Statements for Music Score Collections in Academic Libraries," *Collection
Management* 9 (1987), 69–89. Historical aspects are covered by Carol June Bradley, *American Music
Librarianship: A Biographical and Historical Survey* (New York: Greenwood Press, 1990), 9–68, a section entitled "Building Collections," which focuses on the work of Otto Kinkeldey, Carl Engel, Carleton Sprague
Smith, and Harold Spivacke.
3. Simply because of where my experience has taken place, I will focus specifically here on the academic music library, whether in a conservatory or university setting. Such a point of view does not intend
to overlook or slight the important music collections available in the public libraries of this country, or
indeed in the great music research collections such as the New York Public Library or the Library of
Congress.

select materials in areas where they have scholarly training—sometimes eliminated. Further, it is far more common today to read that librarians are primarily explorers of and guides to electronic and Internet resources than it is to read that librarians are stewards of the human intellectual record. The latter can seem painfully old-fashioned and insufficiently proactive in the so-called "information age" (though I will argue that the role of steward of the human intellectual record is more—rather than less—important in the digital age).

This downgrading of collection development, with its historic interest in developing collections of books and journals, is directly related to a series of myths that appeared and for the most part disintegrated in the last two decades of the twentieth century. The first myth was that books (and print media generally) were soon to disappear, and with them the concept of the library as storehouse for such materials. In this myth, all past writings would be digitized, and, as the common wisdom had it, one could have the entire intellectual content of the Library of Congress on a few CD-ROMs. While digitization brings with it enormous potential for certain classes of materials, we have since realized that from the point of view of long-term preservation, the printed book or journal (sometimes necessarily reformatted on acid-free paper) is at present a more stable medium than is the digital document.

In a related myth, given digital information and the concomitant reduced need for traditional books and libraries, librarians would, of course, no longer work in libraries and with collections. Rather, they would be information brokers who would search the Internet on behalf of their clients, providing information more than engaging with the processes of teaching and scholarship.

Allied with these two myths was that of access rather than ownership—the notion that libraries could focus less than heretofore on actually housing needed documents. Rather, those documents that could not be obtained directly from the Internet would be purchased for the user from a document delivery service or obtained from other libraries. In this myth, ownership of materials—and by implication the traditional functions of collection development—were no longer necessary. The major flaw in the access/ownership debate was the naive belief that those few large research libraries that would continue to collect and catalog would share boundlessly with those libraries on the cutting edge who would invest more and more of their resources in the provision of information and access from electronic resources.

If the tone here seems somehow too pessimistic, even cynical, with respect to the institutional denigration of collection development in some academic research libraries, it is possible to be rather more optimistic when looking at academic music libraries, where music librarians continue to engage in the vital intellectual task of carefully and purposefully building music collections for varying groups of students and teachers, performers and scholars. Because the study of music continues to rely on the interrelated use of three distinct information formats—scores (the notated manifestation of a composer's or improviser's thought), recordings (realizations in sound, and sometimes video, of such compositions and improvisations), and books and journals (intellectual thought regarding such compositions and improvisations)—music libraries continue to require specialized librarians who have the knowledge, training, and experience in both librarianship and music to develop collections that integrate these three information formats appropriately for each institution and each group of users. Thus, while certain trends in the last two decades of the twentieth century have served to downplay the role of collection development from that of Coover's "sacred professional trust," the very nature of music formats tends to demand from music librarianship a continued involvement in and emphasis on collection development.

## THE CHANGING NATURE OF COLLECTIONS

One of the most significant changes in musicological thought of the last two decades is the rejection of the autonomy of music—the notion that music somehow exists in a world of its own, divorced from the larger cultural, intellectual, social, and political world around us.[4] Recently, Nicholas Cook has written:

> Rather than being something apart, music is in the very midst of things. In fact it is less a "something" than a way of knowing the world. . . . You might almost say that music isn't a "something" until, by thinking and writing about it, we turn it into one.[5]

In his first chapter, Cook expands on the role he posits regarding our thinking and writing about music:

> [L]anguage constructs reality rather than merely defining it. And this means that the languages we use of music, the stories that we tell about it, help to determine what music is—what we mean by it, and what it means to us. . . . [W]e have inherited from the past a way of thinking about music that cannot do justice to the diversity of practices and experiences which that small word "music" signifies in today's world. When a book published by

---

4. The essays in Richard Leppert and Susan McClary, eds., *Music and Society: The Politics of Composition, Performance and Reception* (Cambridge: Cambridge University Press, 1987) constitute a significant contribution to debunking the notion of musical autonomy.

5. Nicholas Cook, *Music, A Very Short Introduction* (Oxford: Oxford University Press, 1998), vii.

Oxford University Press a hundred years ago referred to "music," the term had a stability of reference that it no longer has. "Music" meant the European art tradition. . . .[6]

What does this have to do with collection development? If Cook is correct (and I believe that he is), then our thinking, writing, and publishing about music imputes a certain level of meaning to an art that is not, in fact, autonomous—that is, to be discussed only in terms of pitch, rhythm, harmony, counterpoint, form, style, and so on. And the recognition within the last two to three decades that various musics—not only western European art music—are deserving of sustained thought and investigation means that the scope and quantity of writing about music has expanded, and that books and journals in the field have proliferated. It is not that we find quantitatively less thought focusing on repertories of Western art music—it continues apace, even as scholars now think and write about jazz, rock, and a variety of world musics with as much rigor and frequency as that traditionally reserved for the (still vital) repertories of Western art music. We have entered an exciting new era of musical scholarship, one in which newer approaches to thinking and writing about music coexist with more traditional approaches based in the disciplines of archival work, source study, the making of editions, the writing of biography, and so on. In short, it is not a matter of a "newer" type of scholarship *replacing* an "older" type; rather it is an *additive* function in which newer approaches to musical scholarship, as well as the study of a much broader spectrum of musics, makes for a much more comprehensive *construction of musical reality* (to borrow Cook's phrase).

A similar additive phenomenon has occurred in the world of information. The publication of print media—books, journals, and music scores —is thriving. Simultaneously, other information formats, having in common a digital basis, have been added to the more usual array of print: CD-ROM versions of printed reference sources, electronic journals, interactive multimedia, digitized sound or image files. Books and print journals have not been replaced; rather, other information formats have been added to the arsenal of librarians and scholars. Who will lament the passing of the printed *Doctoral Dissertations in Musicology* when *DDM Online* is such a well constructed and easy-to-use World Wide Web resource?[7] Similarly, the electronic journal *Music Theory Online* (*MTO*) co-

---

6. Cook, 14.
7. Cecil Adkins and Alis Dickinson, *Doctoral Dissertations in Musicology*, 7th North American ed., 2d international ed. (Philadelphia: American Musicological Society, International Musicological Society, 1984), and the 2d cumulative ed. that combines the February 1984–April 1995 supplements (Philadelphia: American Musicological Society, International Musicological Society, 1996). *DDM Online:* http://www.music.indiana.edu/ddm.

exists with printed theory journals such as *Journal of Music Theory* and *Music Theory Spectrum*.[8] The one has not replaced the others but rather complements them. Thus, both in the content of music scholarship as well as the information formats that convey that content, what is at work at the turn of the millennium is an additive function that enriches immeasurably both scholarly inquiry and writing.

### SUPPORT FOR BUILDING AND MANAGING COLLECTIONS

If, as I suggest, the "old" (musicology that focuses on western European repertories; print media) is being complemented rather than replaced by the new, then there are implications for resources (fiscal, physical, and human) in the music library. Regarding fiscal resources, much of what Ruth Watanabe wrote in 1981 (excepting the reference to "the uncertain economy") could describe the fiscal environment for higher education and collection development closer to the turn of the millennium:

> During the past several years the uncertain economy has affected library budgets, causing such programs as acquisitions and staff development to suffer. Many libraries have had to accept severe cuts in their annual appropriations for scores, books, and recordings. Even [in] those most fortunate libraries whose budgets have not been sliced, or whose budgets have been augmented, the inflationary costs of materials have so far outdistanced any increase in available funds that they have been deprived of a considerable measure of their purchasing power. The decade of the eighties bids fair to becoming a period of selective collection development.[9]

In spite of a robust American economy during much of the nineties, it was infrequently the case that academic library budgets rose at the rate of inflation for library materials. Thus, just at the moment when music scholarship was becoming diversified and enriched, and just as new (and sometimes expensive) electronic formats appeared in the marketplace, library budgets were providing less in the way of purchasing power. As Watanabe indicated for the eighties, so too for the nineties and as far as reasonably we can see into the early years of the new millennium: in the face of burgeoning scholarship in music we will continue in an era of selective collection development (a term Watanabe uses in contradistinction to the fifties and sixties when several academic music collections

---

8. *Music Theory Online* (*MTO*), the electronic journal of the Society for Music Theory, is accessible at http://smt.ucsb.edu/mto/mtohome.html.

9. Ruth Watanabe, "American Music Libraries and Music Librarianship: An Overview in the Eighties," *Notes* 38 (1981): 252.

came of age).[10] While print media continue to flourish and electronic and digital possibilities proliferate, library budgets on the whole are either stagnating or shrinking.

Compounding these problems is the reality of increasingly limited physical stack space and the sense that substantial campus library buildings with generous space for future growth are, in fact, a thing of the past. Instead, we have entered the era of high-density storage facilities, a reality that serves to underscore the librarian's continual involvement in collection management, particularly in making the difficult but critical distinctions between materials that remain immediately accessible and those that are consigned to a storage facility. Given the continued usefulness of, for example, older opera vocal scores or chamber-music parts, it can be particularly difficult for the music librarian to decide what materials may be relegated to a storage facility. The situation is hardly easier for music books and journals, which, characteristically for the humanities, have a potentially long shelf life. Dan C. Hazen made a fascinating proposal in suggesting that we might deploy our resources for digital scanning in such a way that we focus on enhancing bibliographic records by scanning selectively, e.g., "the title page, the table of contents, and perhaps a page or two of the introduction," thereby providing improved access to off-site resources.[11] The possibility of applying such an enhancement at least to monographic works removed from the music library stacks and consigned to storage is worthy of consideration, thus providing future users with more than just bare bibliographic facts as the only means of judging potential usefulness of items they cannot peruse in the stacks.

There are no easy answers to either fiscal or physical space constraints. It is probably fair to say that we have hardly exhausted the possibilities inherent in regional or statewide cooperation, both for collection development and storage. While neighboring music collections will by definition have a certain degree of overlap in scores, recordings, books, and journals, each can carve out specialty areas in which the other will collect much less intensively. While one may choose a monographic focus on the history of stringed instruments, a neighboring institution may provide complementary coverage in the history of keyboard instruments. While one may focus on a scores approval plan covering North American composers of the last fifty years, another may focus instead on recent British or Austro-German composers of the same time period, the goal

---

10. In truth, even during these decades there were few music libraries that were engaged in something distinctly more than *selective* collection development.

11. Dan C. Hazen, "Making Collections Work: Remote Access and Browsing," *College & Research Libraries News* 59 (1998): 9.

being for each institution to build well-defined collections of significant depth over a sustained time period, the various collections complementing one another in the aggregate.

## REAFFIRMING COLLECTION DEVELOPMENT

The best answer, however, to the dilemma of an expanded world of music in a time of limited fiscal resources is to reaffirm Coover's notion of collection development as a "sacred professional trust," a concept that requires the music librarian to be arbiter of the old and the new—both in the content of music and musical scholarship, and in the various formats of information media. Collection development as a way of identifying and acquiring intellectual content now includes, for example, selection of Web-based resources. Some of these resources will be available without charge and will need only to be placed on an individual library's homepage for ready access by that library's user group. Still, collection development demands that such choices be made so that we as music librarians may combine print and digital resources as we interpret the world of music composition, performance, and scholarship for our users.

The music librarian as collection developer will use limited resources to shape collections carefully and thoughtfully, with due regard for the needs of the local user group, the potential for regional cooperation, the necessity of identifying collection strengths and building those areas particularly well, new possibilities in electronic and digital information, and vital new directions in music composition, performance, and study. Only the music librarian as collection developer can shape the collection in terms of a conceptual continuum that (at least for some repertories) moves from primary sources of compositions (whether in the form of facsimiles, digitized images on the Web, or microfilm), to printed scores (perhaps in a whole range of editions), to recorded manifestations (in audio, video, or both), to critical thought (in print media or in digital form). Now more than ever we need to embrace careful collection development as a means toward fostering music study in its broadest dimensions and in the optimum combination of print and digital media.

# PRESERVATION

By John Shepard

––––––––––––––––––––––––– ◇ –––––––––––––––––––––––––

It has been a century of destruction unparalleled in human history, but the twentieth has been *the* preservation century for libraries. Awareness of the problem of the acidity of mass-produced paper became widespread only by the 1950s, even though the roots of the problem were in the mid-nineteenth century; concerted national efforts to deal with the problem had to wait until the 1980s. While the problem with the medium of paper (the principal means—other than performance—of disseminating music until sound recording became viable in the 1930s) had its origins in production methods using wood pulp developed around 1840, new media created during the twentieth century—various kinds of film, tape, and discs produced from natural and synthetic materials—also began to exhibit preservation problems in succession as they aged, and much more quickly than had wood-pulp paper. It is a testament to the determination and ingenuity of humankind that the twentieth century has also witnessed the development of technological solutions to the problem of preserving documents on paper and the implementation of these remedies on a vast international scale. Analysis of the chemical composition of brittle paper ultimately led to the development of permanent paper, which, after the patient insistence of librarians, came to be used by book publishers and, ultimately, music publishers. Development of techniques for neutralizing the acid in individual leaves of paper in aqueous solutions led to technologies in which entire collections of bound volumes could be deacidified using vapor in a sealed chamber. Realization of the extent of the problem of brittle paper (25 percent of all volumes in U.S. research libraries in 1988, with more becoming brittle each year) led to nationally funded preservation reformatting programs that created microfilm masters for tens of thousands of titles printed between 1840 and 1950, while the existence of these masters was recorded in international bibliographic utilities to discourage costly duplication of preservation efforts.

Of course, music librarians have often had to demand exceptional treatment for the manuscript and printed repertoires under their care. Microfilm is an adequate, if somewhat less convenient, medium for text,

John Shepard is the curator of rare books and manuscripts in the Music Division of the New York Public Library for the Performing Arts and is a former chair of the MLA Preservation Committee.

12

but musical scores need to be portable—carried to the music stand or the sound archive—for full advantage to be taken of them. Some institutional preservation programs have accommodated the need for hardcopy of music editions by spending the additional funds necessary to produce copyflow at the end of the microfilming process. Even in this instance, however, vigilance by music librarians is essential at every step of preparation of the hardcopy for return to the shelf: commercial binders have been known to place the spine of a newly bound copyflow piano-vocal score in the upper margin so that the end result could not be used by an accompanist.[1] This problem associated with copyflow, along with the impracticability of producing printouts of microfilm frames on both sides of a sheet, motivated the development in the 1980s of a method for making acid-free preservation photocopies which commercial firms (such as the late, lamented Booklab) could supply to libraries lettered and properly bound (i.e., to lie open on the music stand). While the preservation photocopy process lacked microfilming's byproduct—the preservation master negative—the durable scores produced thereby have served most of the needs of conservatory and research library music collections.

Music librarians have not only had to demand that preservation programs be adapted to serve the specific needs of music, but they have also called attention to preservation problems nearly unique to music. Standard library shelving units can accommodate volumes the height and width of standard sheet music editions, but with the development of the orchestra since the middle of the nineteenth century, many scores have been issued in editions which fall into the extreme oversize category. Too often, such scores have been perched on standard library shelves so that they protrude into aisles, inviting collision by library users and book trucks pushed by library staff. Happily, an increasing number of vendors of library furniture are responding to the needs of music libraries by designing shelving units that can accommodate oversized scores lying flat, with many shelves spaced closely so that storage and retrieval are convenient and entail no harm to the scores. In addition, conservation suppliers have developed standard sizes of protective enclosures that can house oversized scores and sets of performance parts, which, because of the way they are used, cannot be bound. Indeed, the ways in which music is used present an additional array of preservation problems. Because large-ensemble music requires multiple copies of

---

1. See the humorous—but true—example in Jane Gottlieb, "Working Against the Odds: Preservation Approaches in a Conservatory Library," in *Knowing the Score: Preserving Collections of Music*, comp. Mark Roosa and Jane Gottlieb, MLA Technical Reports, no. 23 (Canton, Mass.: Music Library Association, 1994), 23.

instrumental parts, materials for unpublished works—and some published ones—were duplicated from manuscripts by the ozalid process in
the era before photocopying could produce legible parts. Since the
process depended upon the use of ammonia, the reproductions were unstable, so that with time either the paper became brittle or the music notation faded. Composers used ozalid reproductions for scores as well, because it allowed them to give copies to conductors while retaining the
master copy. Many such scores found their homes on the shelves of music libraries and were the only access music library users had to certain
unpublished compositions. In New York State, a recent cooperative program specifically targeted ozalid-reproduced scores for photocopy
preservation by commercial vendors.

   In addition to modes of duplication, the actual use of performance
materials creates preservation problems that other types of library holdings do not share. Scores and parts in performance collections are subject to repeated markings and erasures, the exigencies of performance
result in tears and mending by questionable methods, and outdoor performances subject materials to sun, wind, rain, insects, and bird drop-
pings. Those who manage performance collections often scoff at these
problems—the materials are meant to be used as long as they can be,
and then replaced. But music librarians have been arguing with orchestral librarians (in this country, at least, the two groups have their own
professional associations) that there is a time in the life of performance
parts when they become sources that document historical facts, period
performance practice, or a particular version of an orchestral or stage
work. The eminent orchestra librarian Robert Sutherland has called attention to an orchestral part in his library in which a player noted the ex-
act beat of a measure of *La forza del destino* during which the baritone
Leonard Warren collapsed and died on the stage of the Metropolitan
Opera in 1960. At the 1995 meeting of the American Musicological
Society in New York City, Benjamin Marcus Korstvedt delivered a paper
on the authentic version of Bruckner's Fourth Symphony that had been
discounted by editors of "critical" editions of his symphonies.[2] Korstvedt
noted that Bruckner supervised the preparation of a performance of
the authentic version of the Fourth by the Vienna Philharmonic under
Hans Richter and that the version featured many additional lines in the
woodwinds not found in the Haas or Nowak editions of the symphony.
During the question period, an intrigued member of the audience asked
Korstvedt if there was a recording of the version. Robert Bailey volun-

---

2. Since published as Benjamin Marcus Korstvedt, "The First Published Edition of Anton Bruckner's
Fourth Symphony: Collaboration and Authenticity," *19th Century Music* 20 (1996): 3–26.

teered the information that the old monaural Knappertsbusch/Vienna Philharmonic recording conformed to the authentic version, because Knappertsbusch inherited Richter's set of parts. Clearly, that is a set of parts that has achieved the status of source material! It is fortunate that through its joint committee, MLA has built a bridge to the Major Orchestra Librarians' Association, because music librarians must continue to press the argument for the selective preservation of parts.

I have so far confined this mini-overview of the Preservation Century to the problems of music set down on paper, because paper conservation and the reformatting of documents created on paper are the resounding successes of preservation technology and methodology in the twentieth century. Few music librarians, given adequate funding, would have difficulty developing a list of preservation options for a collection of printed or manuscript music. Information resources abound, and standards for methods and materials have been widely promulgated and adhered to. Even if local funding is inadequate, funding agencies have long had the means to evaluate proposals for grants to preserve collections of music on paper.

Ironically, the development of a spectacular new technology toward the century's end may prevent music librarians from capitalizing on the progress made so far with earlier technologies. That new technology is, of course, digitization. Abby Smith, Director of Programs for the Council on Library and Information Resources, has written that digitization raises high expectations of benefits "that can be illusory. . . . One such false expectation—that digital conversion has already or will shortly replace microfilming as the preferred medium for preservation reformatting—could result in irreversible losses of information."[3] That is a pretty strong statement coming from a representative of the organization which is the "administrative home" of the Digital Library Federation, but her reasoning is compelling. Properly produced silver halide microfilm can be expected to last centuries under optimum storage conditions, and it can be read by means of a relatively simple device. Digital information is now stored on a variety of physical media whose durability is unknown (some, like DAT tape, have a life span already known to be short) and it requires a complex interaction of hardware and constantly updated software to be viewed, read, or heard. Yet when the hardware and software are coordinated, access to information, images, and sound files is so quick and vivid that the technology is amazingly seductive—so seductive that we already see some research libraries diverting funds

---

3. Abby Smith, *Why Digitize?* (Washington, D.C.: Council on Library and Information Resources, 1999), iv. This document is also available at the council's Web site, http://www.clir.org.

from tried-and-true preservation programs to costly projects for mounting images or sound clips from their collections on their Web sites. A homepage with images and sound clips enhances the public image of a library, so it is easy to justify funding Web-site development, even if the cost is high. By comparison, spending even limited amounts of money for preservation microfilming or for upgrading environmental systems in a repository are distinctly unattractive propositions. With few exceptions, our library patrons believe in digitization as a panacea. Recently, I spoke with a potential donor of a collection of unpublished disc recordings from the 1940s; he proposed that in exchange for the donation, my library could supply him with copies of the recordings on DAT tape, so that he could enjoy the recordings for years to come. My arguments that DAT tape is a transfer medium, not a preservation medium, fell on deaf ears. My hope for the immediate future is that music librarians, with the help of organizations such as the Council on Library and Information Resources, will constantly enlighten their administrators with realistic assessments of the promise of digitization.

But what are our long-range preservation challenges? Again I quote Abby Smith:

> The next century's major preservation challenge will be to cope with the fragile media of the present century, from magnetic tape to digital files. The record of the twentieth century exists on many media that are far more fragile than paper. From the earliest methods of recording images and sound, such as nitrate film and wax cylinders, to the more contemporary formats of videotape and audio cassette, the media that carry the nontextual information of this century will present future scholars and librarians with more difficult access and preservation decisions than any yet faced with acid paper.[4]

It is obvious that a large portion, if not the majority, of these fragile media are devoted to music in recorded form. It is also obvious that sound archivists have been aware of this problem for some time. So, why is there no national effort to preserve our recorded musical heritage comparable to the federally funded microfilm projects of the Brittle Books Program? The answer lies beyond recent considerations of the political nature of Congressional funding. In the past, funding agencies have been able to evaluate proposals for preserving paper-based collections because of widely accepted principles and standards. In a talk before the Music Library Association at its 1997 annual meeting in New Orleans, Peter S. Graham referred to the absence of principles and standards in the discussions of preserving recorded music. In dwelling on the issue of "migration" of recorded music from one physical medium to another, he

---

4. Abby Smith, *The Future of the Past: Preservation in American Research Libraries* (Washington, D.C.: Council on Library and Information Resources, 1999), 13. This document is also available at the council's Web site, http://www.clir.org.

said there must obviously be technical standards, but also quality-control standards, though these will be debatable: should every imperfection in the source medium (such as scratches on a disc) be transferred to the preservation medium, or should it sound "better" than it would have to those who first listened to the source medium? Graham also asked music librarians what should be saved: should we move all of our old recordings to CD-ROM (if technical assessments were to deem that a viable preservation medium) or let current demand dictate our selection decisions?[5]

Graham concluded his paper by saying that music librarians' solutions to these problems would provide guidelines and precedents for the larger digital community. This statement was very flattering to our profession, but the problem is probably too large for music librarians and sound archivists to solve on their own. We are talking about, after all, the legacy of our international musical culture, much of which (for example, many vernacular repertories) survives only in recorded form. In the 1980s, the Commission on Preservation and Access (now a division of the Council on Library and Information Resources) convened task forces of scholars in a number of disciplines (history, philosophy, medieval studies, etc.) to inform them of the extent of the brittle-book problem and to facilitate their deliberations in developing preservation priorities for their respective areas of study. Because everything cannot be saved, there must be guidelines for deciding what *should* be saved. If such an approach were to be attempted for music in recorded form, I believe the net would have to be cast more broadly. Of course, scholars—musicologists and ethnomusicologists—should be involved, but somehow those who create and recreate music should also have a role in developing guidelines for selecting recorded music for preservation.

First, they need to learn that there is a problem. While much recent news coverage has been given to the preservation problems of Hollywood films, the general music-listening public and the professional music community are largely unaware of the problem of preserving recorded music. For example, in 1993, National Public Radio broadcast an interview with composer Mikel Rouse and members of his Broken Consort, a ensemble which had released some recordings. In describing their performances of Rouse's complex rhythmic patterns, the performers mentioned that verbal instructions often replaced music notation in their rehearsals because traditional notation serves Rouse's musical ideas poorly. Rouse's refusal to find notational solutions in order to produce scores of his music does not necessarily indicate his lack of interest in

---

5. Paraphrased from "Something There Is That Doesn't Love a Wall: Networks, Libraries, and the 21st Century," Plenary Session 3, MLA 66th Annual Meeting, New Orleans, 1 February 1997.

passing his works down to future generations. It is more likely that his attitude indicates an absolute faith in the permanence of sound recordings.

Abby Smith wrote that "digitization is not preservation—at least not yet."[6] Professionals in the recording industry and in sound archives still have high hopes that one of the media that carry digital code may come to serve as the ideal receptacle for our recorded musical heritage. For the future, we can expect that the efforts of the Association of Recorded Sound Collections (ARSC) and cooperating associations will come to fruition so that national or international technical standards for the transfer of recordings from unstable to stable media will be developed and endorsed. But preservation measures that follow such standards will require time, trained staff, and equipment. Because of the sheer size of the recorded musical heritage that is at risk and the limited resources available to libraries, the principle of triage must be applied: decisions must be made about what to preserve and what to allow to deteriorate. These decisions will necessarily balance perceptions of which media are in most imminent danger of deterioration with judgments about which performances of which repertories are most important to preserve.

Consequently, even if technological solutions to the problem of preserving sound recordings are developed in the very near future, the decisions about what to preserve will depend on judgments of the *intellectual content* of recordings. While sound archivists have devoted much research to the nature of deteriorating media, the focus on technical issues has often meant that the intellectual content of sound recordings has evaded consideration. In a number of institutions, sound archives exist independently from music libraries, so that music is just one part of a collection that also contains spoken-word recordings, sound effects, bird calls, and so forth, and the issue of the intellectual content of recordings becomes further fragmented.

Even if political developments in the twenty-first century result in the restoration of vast funds to the National Endowment for the Humanities, its Office of Preservation will still lack the means to evaluate proposals for preserving recorded music. When the time comes that ARSC and the rest of the community of audio preservationists agree on technical standards, the musical community must be ready with the intellectual priorities needed to shape credible preservation proposals. In the proactive spirit of its Plan 2001, my hope for the new century is that MLA will spearhead an effort by the learned societies and professional associations in the field of music to develop these priorities.

---

6. Smith, *Why Digitize?*, 3.

# CATALOGING

## By A. Ralph Papakhian

———————————————————◇———————————————————

The major developments in library music cataloging during the recent past are the result of the application of computer and networking technologies and the corresponding organizational efforts to promote cooperative cataloging in that environment. These developments include the promulgation of *AACR* (and *AACR2*), the implementation of the MARC music format, the OCLC and RLG (RLIN) networks, and the NACO-Music Project. Despite significant and even extraordinary improvements in both the quantity and quality of music cataloging, we are now confronted by numerous dichotomies: requests for enhanced catalog information (additional contents and analytics) vs. calls for simplification; more cooperative cataloging vs. decreases in staffing; improved catalog access vs. outsourcing; standardization vs. recourse to idiosyncratic database construction; basic catalog access vs. information retrieval schematics; MARC vs. metadata. These and other topics will be explored below.

Music cataloging was transformed with the implementation of the MARC music format[1] by the Online Computer Library Center (OCLC) in 1978. Despite previous efforts at encouraging cooperative cataloging and catalog-data exchange (most notably the distribution of Library of Congress catalog cards, the *National Union Catalog*,[2] and the *Music Library Association Catalog of Cards for Printed Music, 1953–1972*),[3] OCLC's implementation was the single most important advance in this regard. Based on standardized cataloging rules (*AACR*)[4] and the utilization of networked computer resources, cooperative cataloging for music materials became a reality: cataloging created at one OCLC institution could be used instantaneously by another. This development was continued by similar implementations at the Research Libraries Group (RLG) in 1980 and the Library of Congress in 1985.

---

A. Ralph Papakhian is head of technical services in the William and Gayle Cook Music Library, Indiana University.

1. *Music, a MARC Format: Specifications for Magnetic Tapes Containing Catalog Records for Music Scores* (Washington: Library of Congress, 1976).

2. *National Union Catalog: Music, Books on Music, and Sound Recordings* (Washington, D.C.: Library of Congress, 1973–89).

3. Elizabeth H. Olmsted, *Music Library Association Catalog of Cards for Printed Music, 1953–1972: A Supplement to the Library of Congress Catalogs*, 2 vols. (Totowa, N.J.: Rowman and Littlefield, 1974).

4. *Anglo-American Cataloging Rules* (Chicago: American Library Association, 1967).

As of July 1999, the OCLC database included 1,312,235 bibliographic records for sound recordings (of which the Library of Congress created 153,382). These bibliographic records represented collective holdings of 14,086,298 sound objects. Music was represented by 923,295 bibliographic records (of which the Library of Congress created 55,328), with holdings totaling 7,476,767. Combining the sound recordings and the scores, the OCLC database included 2,235,530 bibliographic records representing 21,563,065 objects (granted that some proportion of the sound is spoken rather than musical). The OCLC WorldCat database is certainly the largest such database of music materials in the world.

As of August 1999, the RLG/RLIN bibliographic files included 1,529,776 catalog records for scores and 1,814,179 records for sound recordings (totaling 3,343,955 records, which do not necessarily represent unique titles). Even though there is considerable duplication between the OCLC and RLG databases, we can reasonably conclude that the two databases combined provide cataloging data for at least 3,000,000 music score and sound recording items. Cataloging records for music materials are also accessible via several commercial enterprises and from libraries that create such records locally but do not routinely distribute them to central databases. These rather remarkable statistics are presented without regard to the cataloging of other music-library formats (primarily books, serials, microforms, and video recordings).

In addition to bibliographic records, the NACO-Music Project has created 43,417 name or name/title authority records as of September 1998 (with 11,859 modifications to previously existing authority records). The Library of Congress has created thousands of authority records as a result of its normal cataloging activity. And the Library of Congress in a joint project with OCLC has automatically generated over 60,000 machine-derived authority records.

Building on the successes of these cooperative ventures (OCLC, RLG, and the NACO-Music Project), the Program for Cooperative Cataloging (PCC) has recently initiated similar programs for the creation of music bibliographic records coded as fully authorized (BIBCO) and also for the cooperative contribution of music subject terms appropriate for Library of Congress Subject Headings (SACO). These efforts may have a positive impact on the music cataloging environment within the foreseeable future if there is an increase in high-quality, shareable catalog data.

We should not overlook a significant and unique accomplishment of the music library community. The retrospective conversion of the card catalogs of several large academic music libraries in the 1980s and the 1990s was undertaken under the auspices of the Associated Music Libraries Group with funding provided by the Department of Education

Title II program. This enabled and expedited the conversion of numerous other library music collections—a feat not duplicated in other disciplines.

Readers unfamiliar with cataloging techniques prior to the use of computers and networks will find it difficult to appreciate the full impact of these technologies on day-to-day work. The cataloger's former armament of typewriters, card stock, pens, pencils, exacto blades, erasers, correction fluid, and so forth, supported by vigorous exercise resulting from constant walking around the library in order to verify information in card and printed catalogs, has been gradually replaced by the sedentary perusal of computer screens, the tapping of computer keyboard keys, complaints about network down time, and, eventually, unbelievable access to a universe of information by means of a few clicks on a World Wide Web browser. This process has accelerated recently as a result of enhancements in personal computers along with the decline in their cost. Mundane routines associated with the physical handling of cataloging cards have been eliminated, and computer-screen manipulation programs have automated routine manual functions involved in searching, verification, copying and pasting data, and so on. The once-heralded promises for the application of artificial intelligence to the cataloging routine (e.g., automated subject analysis or classification), however, have not materialized.

Despite these truly amazing developments in the bibliographic control of music materials, music cataloging and the bibliographic control of music continue to play second fiddle in the library world. It is apparent that the over three million bibliographic records now included in OCLC's WorldCat and RLG databases, in fact, represent only a fraction of existing musical artifacts. It is relatively easy to calculate the publication of well over ten million pieces of printed music.[5] The universe of sound recording publication is essentially unknown but certainly well over the 1.3 million represented in OCLC. (Several hundreds of thousands of early recordings are represented in the *Rigler and Deutsch Record Index*,[6] now to be supplemented by the *American Vintage Record Labelography*.) And the universe of manuscript music and unpublished sound recordings is, obviously, vast. *RISM Series A/II: Music MSS after 1600*, as a separate *RISM Online* database, represents a major effort at cataloging over two hundred thousand manuscripts from ca. 1600–1850. It is particularly noteworthy because it is now presented in a Web-based version

5. D. W. Krummel, *The Literature of Music Bibliography: An Account of the Writings on the History of Music Printing & Publishing* (Berkeley, Calif.: Fallen Leaf Press, 1992), 69.

6. *Rigler and Deutsch Record Index* (Syracuse, N.Y.: Mi-kal County-Matic, 1983).

7. *RISM Online*, http://www.rism.harvard.edu/rism/DB.html.

that includes music incipits.[7] But what proportion of all published and unpublished music materials have ever found their way into libraries? Some categories of music documents have been collected and deposited in libraries—large sheet music collections, for example, mostly poorly cataloged and indexed. Vast areas of material musical culture have simply been lost either because they have not been collected or preserved, or, if collected and placed in libraries, because they have not been controlled by means of a cataloging process.

Simultaneous with the extraordinary accomplishments represented by cooperative cataloging and OCLC, library administrators have been known to express concerns regarding the cost of music cataloging relative to monographic (book) cataloging. In this regard, the music library community has been unsuccessful in communicating the difficulties or requirements of music cataloging relative to books and periodicals. And there continues to be a prejudice against music in libraries. Though electronic resources have been in existence for quite some time now (since 1925, in the form of sound recordings), such resources did not become fashionable in libraries until those resources were essentially textual (CD-ROMs, electronic journals, and various Web-based documents). While we in the music library community quietly and inexplicably concur with administrative wisdom that the cost of cataloging a few hundred thousand pieces of sheet music or 78-rpm discs is "prohibitive," it is also true and apparently acceptable that the OCLC database includes 33,345,846 bibliographic records for books representing some 661,599,909 books held by participating libraries!

Concomitantly, assumptions regarding the processing of music materials seem to be based on the favored library formats (books and textual electronic sources). The library community in general gives little consideration to the distinguishing features of music objects (numbers of titles per recording, existing indexing sources, number of significant contributors, etc.). Music librarians and MLA have struggled to provide additional analytical access in our library catalogs for music materials because of the lack of reliable external indexing sources for music and sound recordings.

A current dichotomy associated with book cataloging also surfaces in music cataloging: a reduction in personnel in cataloging but a desire to increase access by enhancing descriptions with detailed contents notes and controlled access points. There seems to be a perception in certain circles that no human involvement is required for the cataloging process, that automated systems will supply adequate cataloging data and integration of that data into local library catalogs. Presumably, automation will also provide the enhanced access now expected by library clientele. I remain somewhat skeptical. While efficiencies will be achieved because of the enormous success of shared cataloging as well as OCLC's TechPro entry into the arena of contract cataloging,[8] enhanced access will continue to require the work of local music cataloging professionals —at least in music libraries with collections and budgets of a certain size.

Analysis of locally held materials has long been a service provided by music librarians and continues to be so today. The analysis can be of collections not included in normal cataloging work operations (large gift or purchased collections, sheet music, 78-rpm recordings, etc.) or of various published collections (notably, song anthologies of various kinds). Once again, there is a perception that inclusion of such cataloging within the standard catalog is somehow beyond possibility. The current response to this phenomenon is to create separate databases for each such category of material, databases which are not included in what would be regarded as the national bibliographic database of record (OCLC and RLIN). Again, we see a dichotomy, an opposition between the historical trend of creating a centralized, national, and standard bibliographic database and the newer trend of creating local databases of materials, which for some reason are deemed unworthy of being included in the central database. This may be for reasons of cost or an assumption that all databases of library materials will be easily searchable in a networkwide search. The question, of course, is whether these databases will be interoperable (a fashionable term in the late 1990s) and interaccessible. These are technical possibilities, certainly. But I wonder if we are in the process of creating a network so complicated that it will become impossible to reconstruct it when it fails or even to use it with any degree of confidence as a resource-discovery mechanism.

The application of computer technology on a network level was accompanied by the development of the sophisticated local Online Public Access Catalog (OPAC), which gradually evolved into the Integrated Library System (ILS) and Web-based Public Access Catalog (WebPAC). (I will use "ILS" to mean all three.) These local computer applications, along with the utilization of the revolutionary personal computer, have also contributed to the complete transformation of library cataloging work during the course of the last three decades. Catalog data is now delivered to the information-hungry public immediately upon completion of the processing of materials (and often even before). Tracking of material from selection and ordering to shelf availability is recorded and displayed. Cataloging processes have been modified to take advantage of personal-computer capabilities in relation to ILSs delivered from

8. See "The OCLC TechPro Service," http://www.oclc.org/oclc/promo/6171tech/6171tech.htm.

centralized servers. (Gary Strawn's *Cataloger's Toolkit* has become a model for automatic verification as well as automatic generation of authority records.)[9]

Interestingly enough, however, ILSs in both technical- and public-service views have been designed in a chaotic environment, without any requirements for standard displays and features other than a minimum capability to import and export records in the USMARC communications format (now called MARC21). Some librarians would argue that this competitive and commercial process would necessarily result in the development of the most effective systems. But other librarians will observe that many of the successes and efficiencies of American librarianship have resulted from standardization rather than competition. The hurly-burly of OPAC design has resulted in a situation where a library reader can move from library to library (physically or via the Internet) and be confronted with dozens of different catalog display systems and retrieval techniques. Even installations of the same vendor's system will appear and function differently because of local customization. At the same time, no system seems to be able to apply known sorting standards such as the *ALA Filing Rules* or *Library of Congress Filing Rules*.[10] Few systems seem to understand the function of authority records. The net result has been the birth of a new minor industry associated with implementing the ANSI/NISO Z39.50 standard in order to overcome the obstacles created by the proliferation of incompatible ILSs. The same situation holds for library personnel using the technical-services modes of ILSs: catalogers now are frequently using multiple systems simultaneously with different searching and editing techniques, different indexing, and so forth. How this state of affairs has contributed to efficiencies for library readers and employees is quite difficult to understand. One might even conclude that librarians have failed professionally in this regard—failed to impose standards on ILSs in order to insure interoperability, ease of use by the clientele, and efficient internal library operations—including cataloging. This situation also describes another dichotomy—namely, the apparent desire by Web-savvy librarians to have single portals or gateways into the library information environment, in opposition to the proliferation of multiple commercial systems with different indexing and retrieval techniques.

The proliferation of special databases and the extreme interest in local customization of ILS public displays on the part of public-service librari-

---

9. See Dorothy Van Geison, "User's Guide to Accompany CLARR, the Cataloger's Toolkit," http://www.library.nwu.edu/clarr/home.html.

10. *ALA Filing Rules* (Chicago: American Library Association, 1980), and John C. Rather and Susan C. Biebel, *Library of Congress Filing Rules* (Washington, D.C.: Library of Congress, 1980).

ans and administrators is certainly novel. This new interest in the display of electronic catalog data is remarkable in light of a previous lack of interest in the card-catalog environment. The condition known as "cataloger envy" has been identified in the literature to account for this phenomenon.[11] Prior to the appearance of the OPAC, the card catalog was the exclusive domain of the cataloger. Once the OPAC or ILS became visible beyond the card catalog room, everyone seemed to want a hand in designing the system and "interface."

The publication of AACR in 1967 coincided with the first experiments with machine-readable cataloging (MARC). The continued development of both, by gradually incorporating different library materials on the basis of principles and international standards (for example, the International Standard Bibliographic Description [ISBD]), has enabled cooperative cataloging. Despite centrifugal tendencies to sway, the dominance of the rules and the MARC format continues to encourage standardization in library cataloging and technical processing. The publication of AACR also led to considerable research in catalog theory. The implementation of MARC was one of the first large-scale applications of computerized information storage and retrieval.

Future developments in music cataloging are likely to be incremental, unless digital storage and retrieval of recorded and notated music become prevalent quickly. Considerable and fascinating theoretical work on catalog design is underway, focusing on relational database construction, access authority records, bibliographical relationships, and information-retrieval structures. It is unclear how this work will be applied in libraries given the chaotic state of ILSs, the deliberate reduction of cataloging staff, and the inability of existing systems to meet simple catalog objectives (e.g., to clearly display what works a library has by a composer). If current ILSs met basic catalog objectives outlined more than a century ago,[12] collectively we might be more optimistic about transforming catalogs into sophisticated informational-retrieval systems in order to enable clientele to exploit library materials more fully.

My pessimism in this regard would not change dramatically if the digital revolution were to become reality in music. Such a revolution would truly force a migration of library cataloging from AACR and MARC to different metadata or meta-information indexing systems. But at least as currently described, metadatabases can be created automatically by using

---

11. Ralph Papakhian, "From the Chair," *Music OCLC Users Group Newsletter*, no. 61 (August 1995): 1.

12. "Cutter's objectives." See *Public Libraries in the United States of America: Their History, Condition, and Management*, part 2, *Rules for a Printed Dictionary Catalogue*, by Charles A. Cutter (Washington, D.C.: Government Printing Office, 1876), 10.

computer programs designed to extract technical file details from electronic media. It is questionable whether it will be possible to rely on the creators of digital files to also provide reliable and authoritative metadata that can be utilized in anything approaching an ILS. The consequence is human intervention (as in hiring catalogers and indexers). The costs of human activity in cataloging or metadata creation are unlikely to disappear, unless there is significant decrease in the production of musical objects—an unlikely event.

If the digital revolution does occur in music materials soon, such that the bulk of library-held notated and recorded music is converted into and stored in digital media, then we should expect that our current cataloging practices would be altered significantly. Metadata schemas currently unknown to us will have to be developed to index and control access to the digital data simultaneously. This revolution would open avenues of music research and consultation currently difficult to imagine, but I suspect that these kinds of advances (e.g., creating systems that might search or analyze digital sound files directly in terms of melody, harmony, rhythm, etc.) will not be commercially viable for at least a few decades—again because of labor costs being high relative to any possible financial return.

For the immediate future, some music materials will surely be distributed in digital formats via the Internet. The flurry of current metadata activity has been associated with Internet (primarily Web-accessible) resources rather than with analog objects, except for the creation of finding aids for archival collections. The environment is experimental, with metadatabases popping up here and there. The goal of the single portal or gateway is eroding. I predict that this new Babel of metadatabases and ILSs will eventually lead to a renewed call for simplification and standardization, at least in libraries. And actually, OCLC's Cooperative Online Resource Catalog (CORC) Project is a research project investigating the cooperative creation of Web resources.[13] CORC intends to include and mix metadata for physical and digital items. This will be a brave new world only if existing music library collections and future printed and pressed formats are either converted into digital formats or issued as digital documents. In the meantime, library-catalog access should not be further confounded. It should be made easier to use than it is now with logically ordered search results and clearly designated guides.

    13. See Thomas B. Hickey, "CORC—Cooperative Online Resource Catalog," http://www.oclc.org/oclc/research/publications/review98/hickey/corc.htm.

Improved subject analysis of music materials has continued to gener-
ate interest, with considerable effort being made to create a music thesaurus along the lines of the *Art & Architecture Thesaurus*.[14] It will be some
time before the thesaurus is funded and developed, and some additional
time beyond that before the thesaurus can be applied to existing databases of music library materials. In the meantime, normal subject analysis of library music materials will probably be a continued application of
*Library of Congress Subject Headings*.[15]

Shelf classification of music library materials has not altered remarkably since the last revision of 780 for Dewey in 1979.[16] Most music libraries have been and will continue to use *Library of Congress Classification*
*M*[17] or Dewey 780 for notated music. Some libraries are also using these
schemes for sound recordings, while many simply shelve recordings by
label and label number, or by an accession-number system. Public libraries have developed various broad shelving schemes resembling
record-store bin arrangements. Since physical browsing will be impossible in the digital-library environment, if the digital library materializes, I
would expect to see a renewed interest in systematic classification of digital objects in order to provide virtual browsing.

Finally, I should address the education of future music librarians and
music catalogers. The disappearance of graduate programs in music
librarianship is an extremely serious problem. The general climate in
library and information science education currently discourages professional training in librarianship in favor of training in information science and technology (a.k.a. "Webology"). A formal cataloging course is
required for the master's degree in library science in few of the existing
graduate programs; advanced cataloging is now rarely even offered. This
is the result of an attitude that apparently disregards cataloging as a
professional competency. The situation for music cataloging is also glum.
Important programs offering specialization in music librarianship have
closed (Chicago, Columbia, Geneseo, etc.), and others have reduced education in cataloging considerably (Michigan and Berkeley). The norm
for education in music cataloging is now by means of an internship available at only a few schools. The future market for music librarians and

---

14. Toni Petersen, *Art & Architecture Thesaurus*, 3 vols. (New York: Oxford University Press, on behalf
of the J. Paul Getty Trust, 1990); 2d ed., 5 vols. (New York: Oxford University Press, 1994).

15. *Library of Congress Subject Headings*, 22d ed. (Washington, D.C.: Cataloging Distribution Service,
Library of Congress, 1999).

16. *DDC, Dewey Decimal Classification: Proposed Revision of 780, Music* (Albany, N.Y.: Forest Press, 1980).
See also Richard B. Wursten, comp., *In Celebration of Revised 780: Music in the Dewey Decimal Classification*,
MLA Technical Reports, no. 19 (Canton, Mass.: Music Library Association, 1990).

17. *Library of Congress Classification, M: Music, Books on Music*, 1998 ed. (Washington, D.C.: Library of
Congress Cataloging Distribution Service, 1999).

music catalogers will likely determine the arena for appropriate graduate training.

Musical objects—analog or digital, physical items or electronic files— will not disappear anytime soon. Libraries will continue to collect these objects. There is a remote possibility that all musical objects will be digitized and transmitted via a network unlimited in its capacity to deliver multimedia, textual, and musical data in real time. Otherwise, libraries will continue to serve their historic purposes with respect to music materials—to collect, organize, and provide access for the sake of their respective clienteles and for posterity. The mix of formats will certainly change over time. The basic objectives of cataloging will continue to be essential: description and access of materials "held" by the library in an easily usable catalog so that the clientele (including the library staff) can quickly determine whether the library provides access to a known item (by author, title, or subject), or to determine what works by a given composer, or in a given genre, or about a given subject can be accessed. Keyword indexing is a tremendous bonus. Data mining is a bonus. Mapping interesting bibliographic or authorial relationships is a bonus. It would be nice if the basic objectives were met in the near term at least within the context of a local ILS. I predict that in a decade or so we will see a combination of new forms of description incorporating various metadata systems along with advances in indexing and control of digital documents. If technical and social problems are resolved regarding the distribution of digital musical documents, we may see catalogers hired by publishers in order to create metadata for self-indexing networked objects. Certainly we will see some growth in contract cataloging. These kinds of changes in music cataloging are likely to be evolutionary, just as the transformation of the formats of materials acquired by libraries is likely to be evolutionary as a result of social and economic forces. The digital revolution is real, but probably not as expeditious as predicted by the computer and communications industries.

# TECHNOLOGY

BY H. STEPHEN WRIGHT

◇

In an astonishing 1945 article, scientist Vannevar Bush offered his vision of a marvelous machine he called the "memex."[1] As depicted by Bush, the memex would enable scholars to search a vast repository of scholarly information, take notes, copy information as needed, and create new scholarship—all with incredible speed. One of the most striking features of the memex is what Bush called "associative indexing," in which links can be built between items of information, enabling the scholar to jump from one to another instantaneously—an amazingly prescient vision of what we now call hypertext. Clearly, Bush imagined the scholar's workstation decades before it became a reality.

One factor, however, immediately anchors Bush's memex firmly within the technology of 1945 and casts a faint veneer of quaintness over his bold conception: Bush was not describing a computer, nor anything we would recognize as a precursor of one. Rather, the memex—which was never built—incorporates rolls of microfilm driven by high-speed motors, along with a dry-photography process to copy and store information. No electronic data storage—digital, analog, or otherwise—is involved.

The contrast between Bush's prophetic ideas and the mundane pre-electronic technology within which he framed them provides a dramatic demonstration of the pitfalls of any attempt to forecast the library technology of the next century. Any vision of future technology that is merely an extension of present-day technology may well appear ludicrously dated within a few decades, or even a few years. Science fiction writer Arthur C. Clarke stated that "any sufficiently advanced technology is indistinguishable from magic."[2] A corollary of Clarke's assertion is that in order to retain some semblance of plausibility in any discussion of future libraries, we must extrapolate from the technology of our time. We may readily speculate on what challenges and promises await the music libraries of the next millennium, but must remain aware that all our speculations could be swept away by some unforeseen technological breakthrough.

H. Stephen Wright is music librarian at Northern Illinois University.
1. Vannevar Bush, "As We May Think," *Atlantic Monthly*, July 1945, 101–8.
2. Arthur C. Clarke, *Profiles of the Future: An Inquiry into the Limits of the Possible*, rev. ed. (New York: Harper and Row, 1973), 21.

The last twenty years have seen a tremendous incursion of computer technology into the library world, accompanied by huge triumphs and some equally huge embarrassments. We have converted the monumental card catalogs and other manual bibliographic files into vast shared databases such as OCLC, RLIN, and other consortial catalogs. The grandeur of this achievement, in which music librarians played a significant role, cannot be overstated. Yet, in the constant tendencies of library administrators to devalue cataloging, to treat it as a commodity which must be purchased for the lowest possible cost and without regard to quality, we risk degrading and adulterating this accomplishment.

We have also risked losing the trust of the scholarly world as we packaged our remarkable bibliographic edifices within inferior electronic systems. During the 1980s, when creaky, primitive online catalogs first appeared in libraries, administrators soon began to insist that card catalogs were obsolete and must be abandoned, or even discarded. The flaw in this reasoning is painfully obvious in retrospect; at that time, no online catalog could provide the same level of functionality as a card catalog. Few librarians doubted that online catalogs would eventually supplant manual catalogs; however, by forcing an immature technology on our clientele, we did considerable harm to our own professional reputations as the caretakers of the human record. Nicholson Baker's famous 1994 screed against libraries that were consigning the card catalog to oblivion caused widespread consternation in the library profession, primarily because most of Baker's complaints about online catalogs were devastatingly accurate.[3] Some (but not all) of the flaws Baker enumerated have since been remedied, but the damage has already been done.

Libraries are now repeating this mistake with the so-called "full-text" periodical databases; we now offer our clientele what we misleadingly call "e-journals," a term which implies an equivalence which does not exist. What we are actually offering are indexing services that sometimes (subject, of course, to copyright clearances) supply electronic versions of articles retrieved via author, title, subject, or keyword searches. These electronic versions may be plain ASCII text, stripped of all graphical components; they might be reasonably accurate visual simulations of the original content, utilizing the Adobe Acrobat format; or they might be something in between. With most of these full-text databases, however, one cannot assemble a complete virtual journal issue on the screen. Once again, immature technology is being forced onto the stage unrehearsed and unprepared, and no one is fooled. It remains to be seen whether librarians of the next century will continue this pattern.

---

3. Nicholson Baker, "Discards," *New Yorker*, 4 April 1994, 64–86.

One of the most troublesome aspects of e-journals is that they are invariably offered within self-contained packages from library vendors; before you can read the latest articles from your favorite e-journal, you must determine which vendor offers that particular title. Essentially, we have surrendered control of e-journals to corporate entities—just as we have allowed corporations to design and control our online catalogs—and these corporations can and do unilaterally decide what journals will be included, excluded, added, or dropped.

In music libraries, we are in serious peril of replicating the embarrassment of full-text databases with the current tropism toward electronic distribution of digital audio. Faced with bewildering problems of storage space and licensing, music libraries will inevitably succumb to the temptation to lease collections of digitized audio from commercial enterprises. Undoubtedly this will reduce the stress of absorbing the new audio technology into our collections, but we may also relinquish control over the selection and cataloging of particular works and performances.

Baker also complained of the anti-intuitive nature of online catalog interfaces, and indeed, this is one of the significant failures of library technology: our inability to provide a consistent, logical, intuitive interface for electronic catalogs and reference tools. In the days of card catalogs, one could enter a library anywhere in the United States and be reasonably confident of finding a usable card catalog; one might have found a dictionary catalog (with authors, titles, and subjects in a single alphabet) or some kind of divided catalog, but one could quickly assimilate these variations. Now we present our clientele with a bewildering assortment of interfaces, each with its own frustrating idiosyncracies. Every online catalog and every electronic reference source has its own proprietary interface and search protocols, all apparently designed in willful ignorance of each other. The commands, keystrokes, and icons for initiating searches and moving from one display to another differ wildly between competing systems. Some libraries even offer both text-based and graphical variants of their own catalogs. Surely one of the paramount challenges to twenty-first-century librarians will be to achieve the goal of a seamless, unified, and standard interface—but given the increasing reliance on commercially produced electronic products, this goal seems distant indeed.

The dream of one standard interface to all library catalogs and databases will probably seem like a near-frivolous luxury as other technological pressures drain our energy and resources. In particular, pressure to upgrade equipment and software and convert to progressively more sophisticated and short-lived formats promises to be a constant burden well into the next century. Many libraries have already been through several iterations of online catalogs, starting with command-driven, line-mode systems, progressing through full-screen textual catalogs to graphical interfaces. Each time a new system is introduced, there are inevitable problems of data conversion, equipment compatibility, staff training, and user education (and despite whatever improvements in functionality are obtained in a system upgrade, these transitions win us no friends among our clientele). We breathe collective sighs of relief whenever one of these upgrades is completed, but does anyone really believe that the situation will ever stabilize? A future of massive system upgrades every five to ten years is truly depressing to contemplate.

Yet it is not only library catalogs that become antiquated in absurdly short spans of years. Our collections, the very fabric of our libraries, now face similar perpetual cycles of obsolescence. Most music libraries have long since shifted their sound recording acquisitions to compact discs, and some libraries (particularly public libraries) have even gone so far as to sell or discard their collections of vinyl discs. The Music Library Association has even published an extensive bibliography delineating the contents of a "basic music library," including thousands of compact discs —thus implying, by chance or by design, that a "basic" collection *must* include CD manifestations of all essential works.[4] Yet, hanging over the justifiable celebration of the many advantages of compact discs over LPs is the shadow of an ominous delusion—the delusion that once we have replaced our LP collections, we will never have to do it again.

Of course, we *will* have to do it again; it is merely a matter of time. It might not be this generation of librarians, but if not, certainly the next— and they will not be the last to have to do it, either. Astronomer Clifford Stoll, in *Silicon Snake Oil,* describes how he helped record the precious data from the Pioneer flyby of Saturn in 1979. In order to preserve this priceless scientific data for future generations, Stoll and his colleagues saved it in four formats—nine-track tape, seven-track tape, paper tape, and punch cards—*all* of which are now utterly obsolete.[5] There is no reason to assume that the same will not be true of the standard sound and video recording formats of today.

Libraries that have relegated their LP collections to remote storage facilities, annual book sales, or landfills may claim—quite correctly—that not every library can function as an archive. The music libraries of the next century must find a balance between replacement and preservation, and must endeavor to make this as painless as possible for their clientele,

4. Elizabeth Davis et al., eds., *A Basic Music Library: Essential Scores and Sound Recordings,* 3d ed. (Chicago: American Library Association, 1997).

5. Clifford Stoll, *Silicon Snake Oil: Second Thoughts on the Information Highway* (New York: Doubleday, 1995), 180.

offering them "format neutrality"—equal levels of support and access for at least the last few decades of format changes.

Printed materials will, in all likelihood, continue to be a staple of music libraries. The book is still a remarkably viable piece of technology; furthermore, any practicing musician knows that, despite whatever advantages a digitized score may offer, a printed manifestation of a work is essential for study and performance. The delivery of that printed copy will, however, evolve to take advantage of digital technologies. Publishing-on-demand, in which a single printed copy is replicated from a digitally stored version, is already a reality and will undoubtedly proliferate; a few companies already offer downloadable versions of scores, and certainly more will follow. Music libraries can, and will, be acquiring on-demand printings as part of their normal acquisition procedures; what is less certain is whether libraries will participate in delivery of these digitized books and scores to their clientele. Conceivably a library could purchase an electronic edition of a work and print copies for users as needed—but complex copyright and royalty issues would certainly have to be resolved. As with full-text databases and sound recordings, commercial enterprises will likely emerge to offer licensed libraries of digitized scores—and another substantial segment of the library world will be ceded to the private sector.

In fact, the specter of copyright hovers over every scenario of the electronic library of the future. The fantasy of a fully digitized library is still popular, though the realization of this chimeric dream would require nothing less than the worldwide abolition of intellectual property laws— a political impossibility—as well as unimaginably vast costs associated with scanning the untold millions of printed volumes now residing in our stacks. If, in some distant future, libraries have no printed materials at all, it will not be because they have scanned them and stored them electronically; it will be because they discarded them, allowed them to decay into dust, or never had them in the first place.

Yet, as intimidating as some of these challenges may be, they are ultimately practical, even mundane; upgrading and maintaining equipment, converting data, and educating our staff and our users are all predictable issues involved in assimilating new technology into a library. One area of technological advancement that is far less amenable to prediction is the application of computers to reference work—not in terms of computer-based reference sources, but computers as the *providers* of reference assistance itself. Indeed, anyone who spends an afternoon watching library users at online catalog terminals cannot fail to notice that many users assume that the computer *is* capable of providing assistance; they type queries in natural language, or construct elaborate phrases that have no relationship to controlled vocabulary. They assume that the computer knows that "J. S. Bach" is the same person as "Johann Sebastian Bach," and that "ninth symphony" is equivalent to "symphony no. 9," and react with stunned derision when told that the computer is not necessarily capable of making these simple deductions. We lament these ill-informed assumptions and attempt to counteract them through bibliographic instruction, a process that often feels like shoveling sand against the waves. Yet, as computers grow ever more powerful, should we not consider adapting the system to the user? If they think the computer understands them, perhaps we should make it so the computer *does* understand them.

An intelligent, sentient computer, like the urbane HAL 9000 in Stanley Kubrick's *2001: A Space Odyssey,* is probably not in the immediate future of the library. Despite the well-publicized chess-playing prowess of some computers, a machine that truly thinks (or that gives a convincing illusion of thought, in the manner of the famous "Turing test" of philosopher Alan Turing) is still out of reach. Yet there is no reason why we cannot apply known principles of fuzzy logic and artificial intelligence to library computer systems, and give them the ability to make inferences about what a user probably wants, based on their often ill-formed queries.

The notion of a computer that will replace a reference librarian may seem almost self-destructive, but if we do not do this, it will probably be done for us. Already there are at least two Internet search engines, AltaVista and Ask Jeeves, that invite users to enter their queries in natural language rather than as strings of keywords joined by Boolean operators. It is questionable whether either of these search engines really has the capability of understanding questions, but if users *think* they do, then we are already behind. Many people already treat the Internet as a substitute for the library—even though nothing is evaluated, nothing is selected, nothing is organized, and nothing is excluded—and increasingly, users are turning away from our magnificent bibliographic structures, lured by the illusory friendliness of commercial search tools. Clearly, providing an electronic version of a card catalog—wondrous though that is—may not be enough.

Let us not, though, become too mired in bleak forecasts. If we assume a "best-case" scenario, what would the ideal music library of the future be?

This ideal library would have an electronic catalog with a clear, standardized, self-revelatory interface, offering seamless, unified access to bibliographic data of all kinds, as well as digitized visual and audio information. Catalog users could move effortlessly from bibliographic records to digitally stored versions of items when they are available; locally stored data and information from the Internet (or its eventual successor) would be retrieved with equal ease. The catalog would also guide the user, with ease and encouragement, to physical versions of items when appropriate. The catalog would have expertly maintained bibliographic information —created by humans, not by automated "spiders"—arranged in clear, intuitively browsable matrices, and would offer transparent access to materials outside the library in ever-increasing circles (the regional consortium, the state, the nation, and finally the entire world). The catalog would not be the unforgiving digital imbecile of today; it would interpret user queries, suggest possible headings to search, and fill in missing information as needed.

Collections would offer a sense of continuity; libraries would offer the most current information possible but would also maintain links to the past, through preservation and support of existing materials in older formats. Transitions to new formats and new systems would happen gradually and painlessly. Users could be assured of finding and utilizing the sources they needed—whether score, recording, printed literature, or electronic information—without worries about format or copyright problems. Digitized audio and video stored in local servers and scores and performances retrieved electronically over a worldwide network would coexist peacefully with printed materials and physical sound carriers.

The librarians of this future music library would be free of, or at least better able to cope with, abrupt technological shifts. Librarians could focus on building collections rather than replacing them, contributing to and maintaining their bibliographic databases rather than converting them, and offering in-depth assistance and instruction to their clientele rather than simply offering coping strategies and "work-arounds" for system deficiencies. Finally, the music librarians of the future will continue today's tradition of free access to information of all kinds and in all formats, unencumbered by commercial priorities.

We should remember, however, that like Vannevar Bush's memex, our current notions of the future of library technology may soon seem simultaneously clever and outmoded. As Arthur C. Clarke has said, "the real future is not *logically* foreseeable."[6] Undoubtedly, the next century holds some unexpected technological breakthrough, as impossible for us to imagine as atomic energy would have been to a scientist of the nineteenth century, that will force us to rethink and reinvent our libraries; we can only hope that it will not render us obsolete as well.

---

6. Clarke, 15.

# COPYRIGHT

## By Mary Wallace Davidson

—————————————————— ◇ ——————————————————

Most music librarians have a working knowledge of the United States Copyright Law with respect to situations that arise in the library, especially with respect to the use of musical works captured on paper, recordings, and film. Few at the moment, however, have had to tangle with legal issues of licensing electronic reference sources, storing and streaming digitally formatted sound to computer workstations, or providing library materials legally for distance-learning classes. Fewer still know whether they are Online Service Providers (OSPs), as defined by the Digital Millennium Copyright Act of 1998 (DMCA),[1] and if they are, what rights and responsibilities that definition imposes. As we cope with this, and the many other public laws now so rapidly being sponsored and passed by members of Congress, we risk losing sight of some significant historical threads to guide us into the future.

The United States Constitution provides that "The Congress shall have Power . . . To promote the Progress of Science and useful Arts, by securing for limited Times to Authors and Inventors the exclusive Right to their respective Writings and Discoveries."[2] The framers fortunately understood two conditions necessary for fostering the natural growth of artistic and scientific culture: (1) creative individuals must have some economic incentive to pursue their craft, and (2) their successors must be able to use the results as seeds for new growth while those seeds are still alive.

The first federal copyright law passed by Congress in 1790 protected only published books, maps, and charts for fourteen years, with option for the same period of renewal. Published music was not protected until the first general revision of this law in 1831 (when the first term was extended to twenty-eight years), and dramatic works not until 1856. The second general revision, in 1870, added published works of art and the rights of authors to create certain derivative works. It also centralized deposit and registration in the Library of Congress (rather than with the states). The Copyright Law first protected music in public performances

---

Mary Wallace Davidson is head of the William and Gayle Cook Music Library at Indiana University. She has been a member of the Music Library Association's Legislation Committee since 1990, and from 1995 to 1997 represented MLA at the Conference on Fair Use, sponsored by the U.S. Patent and Trademark Office.
1. *U.S. Statutes at Large* 112 (1998): 2859–918.
2. U.S. Constitution, art. 1, sec. 8.

in 1897 and certain kinds of unpublished works in the third major revision of 1909. Motion pictures (previously registered as photographs) joined protected formats in 1912. Limited federal copyright protection was finally granted to sound recordings (fixed and first published on or after 1972) in the most recent thorough revision of the law in 1976,[3] which also provided for all unpublished works. Computer programs first entered the law at the end of 1980,[4] followed by the Semiconductor Chip Protection Act of 1984[5] and the Computer Software Rental Amendments Act of 1990.[6] The Audio Home Recording Act of 1992[7] clarified the legality of home taping for private use while imposing royalties on the sale of digital audio recording devices.

The law did not concern itself with "moral rights" until 1992,[8] although these often take precedence over copyrights in other countries. Various international agreements have extended protection to works published outside the United States, beginning with the Universal Copyright Convention in 1952. The United States' adoption of the earlier Berne Convention in 1989 had a greater effect, particularly as a result of the World Intellectual Property Organization Copyright Treaty in 1996, to which the United States is also a signatory. The Uruguay Round Agreements Act of 1994[9] restored copyright protection in the United States to certain foreign works that had been protected in the source country (e.g., the former Soviet Union) but not here.

The DMCA and the Sonny Bono Copyright Term Extension Act of 1998 (known as the "Sonny Bono Law")[10] change the law in matters of potentially great significance to libraries.[11] Among other provisions, the DMCA revises section 108 to allow what has been the practice for many years (three preservation copies rather than one), and also specifies that

---

3. "Title 17, USC, Copyrights," *U.S. Statutes at Large* 90 (1976): 2541–602.
4. "Patent and Trademark Laws, Amendment," *U.S. Statutes at Large* 94 (1980): 3028.
5. *U.S. Statutes at Large* 98 (1984): 1727–28.
6. Ibid., 104 (1990): 5134–37.
7. Ibid., 106 (1992): 4237–48.
8. Section 106A, "Rights of Certain Authors to Attribution and Integrity," *Visual Artists Rights Act of 1990, U.S. Statutes at Large* 104 (1990): 5128–30.
9. *U.S. Statutes at Large* 108 (1994): 4973–81.
10. Ibid., 112 (1998): 2827–34.
11. For a clear discussion of the impact of these two laws on libraries, see Arnold P. Lutzker, "Primer on the Digital Millennium: What the Digital Millennium Copyright Act and the Copyright Term Extension Act Mean for the Library Community," at the Web site of the Association of Research Libraries, http://www.arl.org/info/frn/copy/primer.html (last modified 8 March 1999). The effect of the DMCA on section 108 of the Copyright Law regarding library preservation is posted in both "redlined" and "clean" versions of the section at the University of Texas, Office of General Counsel, "Crash Course in Copyright," http://www.utsystem.edu/ogc/intellectualproperty/108.htm, created by Georgia Harper (updated 24 June 1999). A good chart that captures all effects of the Sony Bono Law on term extension was published by Peter B. Hirtle on the last page of a four-page insert, "Recent Changes to the Copyright Law: Copyright Term Extension," *Archival Outlook*, January/February 1999, between pages 22 and 23.

preservation copies may be digital if they remain within the library. Works published before 1923 were unaffected by the Sonny Bono Law, and remain in public domain. The effect of term-extension provisions on works published from 1923 to date is complex, but for works published after 1 March 1989, the act extends protection to 70 years after the death of the author, or if a work of corporate authorship, the shorter of 95 years from the date of publication or 120 years from the date of creation. Some would say these term limits are a far cry from our Constitution's original intent.

Under the current law, "copyright" means just what it says: the creator enjoys the exclusive right to make copies (a term later broadened to include displays, performances, and recordings) of identifiable, reproducible ("fixed") manifestations of creative works that are the intellectual property of their creators for certain limited time periods. The property must be of substantive creative merit to warrant such protection —that is, not just an idea or a title. There are currently exemptions to ("limitations on") these exclusive rights, even during the period of protection, that make creative works available to teachers, scholars, and critics under the four conditions known as fair use or "fair dealing" in other English-speaking countries (sec. 107). Other exemptions apply to libraries (sec. 108), owners of exemplars (sec. 109), performers (sec. 110), broadcasters (sec. 111), and transmitters of ephemeral recordings (sec. 112). The text for the Fair Use exemption (sec. 107, as amended in 1990 and 1992) is the most succinct and oft quoted:

§ 107. LIMITATIONS ON EXCLUSIVE RIGHTS: FAIR USE
Notwithstanding the provisions of sections 106 and 106A, the fair use of a copyrighted work, including such use by reproduction in copies or phonorecords or by any other means specified by that section, for purposes such as criticism, comment, news reporting, teaching (including multiple copies for classroom use), scholarship, or research, is not an infringement of copyright. In determining whether the use made of a work in any particular case is a fair use the factors to be considered shall include—
    (1) the purpose and character of the use, including whether such use is of a commercial nature or is for nonprofit educational purposes;
    (2) the nature of the copyrighted work;
    (3) the amount and substantiality of the portion used in relation to the copyrighted work as a whole; and
    (4) the effect of the use upon the potential market for or value of the copyrighted work.
The fact that a work is unpublished shall not itself bar a finding of fair use if such finding is made upon consideration of all the above factors.[12]

12. *U.S. Code,* Title 17, section 107 (1994, 8:912–13). Justice Sandra Day O'Connor, delivering the opinion of the Supreme Court in *Harper & Roe v. Nation Enterprises,* 471 U.S. 539 (1985), noted that the fourth factor "is undoubtedly the single most important element of fair use." From the same opinion, it is also clear that all four factors must be considered. The final sentence, extending the exemption to unpublished works, was added to section 107 in 1992 (*U.S. Statutes at Large* 106 [1992]: 3145).

The beauty of this section is its very vagueness and lack of specificity. There simply are no answers to fit every case. Rather, the wording suggests only "safe harbors." Interpretation of this section is only possible within a context where both owners and users of intellectual property understand how interdependent they are on each other for the continued health of our culture.

This symbiotic relationship has become quite fragile in the age of digital publication and distribution. If nothing else, the recent Conference on Fair Use (CONFU) confirmed this statement repeatedly throughout the series of meetings beginning in September 1994 and concluding in May 1997.[13] Delegates of some forty (later ninety) organizations—representing authors, publishers, educators, and libraries—were invited to discuss fair-use issues, and "if appropriate and feasible," to develop voluntary guidelines for the fair use of digital works and online services. Hearing little progress, or mention of music, representatives of nineteen music organizations met in April 1996, but the discussion proved equally cautious: "The general consensus was that no change was needed at that time, but that music publishers, music educators, and music librarians would need to be aware of the guidelines being developed by CONFU, which might include uses of music in digital form."[14] In fact, although the *CONFU Report* does contain proposed guidelines for digital images, distance learning, and educational multimedia, none received enough endorsement to be considered consensus, and each was actively opposed by one or more representative groups.

Nevertheless, CONFU had an impact on participants and their organizations, not the least of which was education about the issues involved. Participants were also exposed to concurrent political processes on many levels: local (CONFU as it related to the agenda of the U.S. Patent & Trademark Office), national (Congress), and international (the World Intellectual Property Organization [WIPO]). These venues all had complex "back door" relationships to each other, and still do. CONFU did make a conscious attempt to seek consensus among educators, librarians, and commercial interests. Whereas the educators and librarians clung to the notion that the principles of fair use should remain the same in the digital environment, the commercial interests focused on the fact that digital is different. In a library or a bookshop, one may read a page or two of a book or look at a table of contents or index to see if that book is going to have the information one wants before either

---

13. U.S. Department of Commerce Patent and Trademark Office, *The Conference on Fair Use: Report to the Commissioner on the Conclusion of the First Phase of the Conference on Fair Use,* September 1997 (hereafter, *CONFU Report*). Single copies are available free of charge either from the office, c/o Richard Maulsby, Director, Washington, DC 20231, or via the office's Web site at http://www.uspto.gov.
14. *CONFU Report,* 8.

putting it back, proceeding to acquire it, or making a lawful copy of some portion of it. When that same reader retrieves and displays a digital source for the same purpose, she or he has the capability of transmitting that page—or the entire source—to an infinite number of potential readers, instantly. The commercial representatives at CONFU had not yet calculated how much that difference (and/or convenience) is worth in the marketplace, or how best to ensure a reasonable profit over large costs (nor have they still). So they, too, wanted no change in the Copyright Law at that time. Instead they turned their attention to the international arena.

In spite of its title, the World Intellectual Property Organization concerns itself with international trade (not education or libraries) and is bent on "harmonizing" international laws with respect to the commerce of intellectual property. There were in fact two agreements reached in December 1996: the WIPO Copyright Treaty and the WIPO Performances and Phonograms Treaty. Both, as they say in their preambles, desire to "develop and maintain the protection of the rights [of authors of literary and artistic works, performers, and producers of phonograms] to develop and maintain the protection of [their] rights in a manner as effective and uniform as possible." Both similarly recognize "the need to maintain a balance between the rights [of these authors, performers, and producers] and the larger public interest, particularly education, research and access to information." That said, neither treaty posits any *limitations* to the protected rights in the public interest, except to say that the signatory countries may want to legislate such provisions—but only if these provisions "do not conflict with a normal exploitation of the work and do not unreasonably prejudice the legitimate interests of the [authors, performers, or producers]."[15]

Not surprisingly, there are subtle shifts in the definitions constructed for these treaties, particularly the Performances and Phonograms Treaty, starting with an expanded concept of "phonogram" to include any fixed sound, not just those incorporated in films or audiovisual works. "Fixation" now means "the embodiment of sounds, or of the representations thereof, from which they can be perceived, reproduced or communicated through a device."[16] "Communication to the public," as distinct from publication or broadcasting, means "the transmission to the public by any medium . . . of sounds of a performance or the sounds or the representations of sounds fixed in a phonogram, [and] making [them]

---

15. "WIPO Copyright Treaty," article 10, "Limitations and Exceptions" and the "WIPO Performances and Phonograms Treaty," article 16, "Limitations and Exceptions." Summaries and full texts of both treaties are available through links at http://ecommerce.wipo.int/activities.
16. "WIPO Performances and Phonograms Treaty," article 2.

audible to the public."[17] The language is awkward because it needs to account for present and future technologies (wire, wireless, and so on).

The effect of these international agreements is rapidly becoming pervasive in the European Union and the United States. In the U.S., the DMCA is also known as the WIPO Trade Agreement Implementation Act, in reference to the WIPO Copyright Treaty of 1996, which it seeks to implement. No doubt other legislation will be introduced in future Congresses, and it behooves us all to pay attention. The strength of the commercial interests will unquestionably continue and wax more enthusiastic and powerful as more and more of our culture and its sources of information are digitally packaged and licensed rather than sold. In general, commercial publishers take a dim view of the fair-use argument, seeing it as a dodge from fair reimbursement. Some colleges and universities have been active in exerting their fair-use rights—by establishing written policies, retaining counsel, and so forth—but most of their concerns have been limited to coursepacks and retaining rights of works created by faculty and staff as employees. The educational music community tends either to ignore the fundamental changes in the entertainment industry or to want "a piece of the action." In that case, it wants to be paid for the products it creates, too—if not for profit at least to recoup the heavy start-up costs. These activities will raise thorny legal questions for university counsels.

Licensing is a familiar concept and practice within the music community, as it concerns chiefly performance rights, or rights to use "the work" (or a version of it) as distinguished from a particular manifestation or copy. The concept is now spreading to the digital environment, where publishers want to protect screen displays of electronic resources in educational institutions with the same limitations as "performances or displays" under section 110. From ASCAP, BMI, and SESAC, electronic publishers have also learned the efficacy of a site license. From a creator's or producer's view, it allows centralized and efficient control of contracts and money. Strangely enough, as educational institutions have increasingly adopted business ethics and practices, some administrators have also expressed this same preference for centralization, uniformity, and efficiency on the part of the user as well. The wording of contracts for these licenses is ever hopeful that libraries have the technology to count (report, limit, constrict, etc.) and usually contain such language. Neither the licenses nor the available technology, however, distinguishes the characteristics of a given use of a particular source—that is, whether that use meets the "four factor" test of section 107. In fact, publishers are still

---

17. Ibid.

experimenting and have no rational basis upon which to charge. Music librarians need to watch carefully not only the quality of what they choose to license, but the language of what they choose to sign. Most publishers willingly agree to reasonable changes in contracts, and librarians should not inadvertently put their institutions at legal risk.[18] Nor should they inadvertently put their clients at cultural risk by failing to exercise the rights of fair use and preservation, protected by the Copyright Law of the United States.

Our task for the future is to keep informed about current legislation and to lend our voices to concerted action as appropriate. The Digital Future Coalition (DFC), comprised eventually of some forty-two financially contributing members (including the Music Library Association), was founded in 1995. Because it was "a unique collaboration of many of the nation's leading non-profit educational, scholarly, library and consumer groups, together with major commercial trade associations representing leaders in the consumer electronics, telecommunications, computer and network access industries," it was committed to a balanced approach to legislation, at least through the 105th Congress.[19] The successful passage of the DMCA in fact reflected the credibility of positions taken by the DFC.

Such coalitions may be too good to be true, or at least too expensive to persist, but they are the only possible way to ensure the long-term preservation of our musical culture. Obviously the creators, producers, users, and preservers of music, in all its manifestations, rely on each other's health. Rather than taking myopic positions, it behooves us to talk, understand, educate, and negotiate with one another for the common good. Above all, we must guard against "nickel and diming" the Copyright Law for one special interest after another (including international "harmonization") but not fail to recognize the need for a thorough revision when the time is ripe.

---

18. The Yale University Library maintains a useful site that includes sample license agreements: "LIB-LICENSE: Licensing Digital Information, a Resource for Librarians," http://www.library.yale.edu/~llicense, updated frequently. Yale also hosts a strong statement created by the International Coalition of Library Consortia on "Current Perspective and Preferred Practices on the Selection and Purchase of Electronic Information," http://www.library.yale.edu/consortia/statement.html. A group of six large library associations has mounted "Principles for Licensing Electronic Resources" (final draft, July 1997), http://www.arl.org/scomm/licensing/principles.html.
19. From the DFC's Web site (http://www.dfc.org), last updated in late May 1999. The DFC has apparently ceased to exist since then because of a lack of funding

# REFERENCE

## By David Lasocki

———————————————◇———————————————

After fifteen years in the music reference business, I still find the very idea of reference miraculous. I mean, to have someone highly qualified in the library whose job it is to help you do your research or simply find what you need: isn't that a minor miracle? Like many academics, I stayed clear of reference librarians for years, finding them crabby and haughty when I asked for assistance and in any case believing that I ought to know how to find what I wanted. The turning point for me came in the Guildhall Library, a city archive in London, where the unfamiliarity of the documents required me to consult the astoundingly knowledgeable reference librarian, whose booming voice could be heard the length of the library. Knowing that my business would instantly become public, I timidly approached him one day and explained that I was having trouble reading secretary hand, the standard handwriting style of Elizabethan England. He recommended that I buy a booklet published by the Historical Association and do the exercises in it. I took his advice and, sure enough, within a week I was skimming through secretary hand as if it were Times Roman. As I became more friendly with him, he confided (if that's the right word for his declarations) that he appreciated *real* researchers like me, not those Americans who came over in search of information on their ancestors. Of course, those users were his bread and butter. That was my introduction to what I have come to call the "opinionated reference librarian"[1] as well as to some of the do's and don'ts of reference work (educate your users; don't denigrate any of your other users; keep your voice low).

Wait, you may say: isn't he supposed to be talking about music reference in the year 2000? Well, I am, indirectly. Because I think one critical question we have to face today is whether we will, and should, have highly qualified reference librarians sitting at a desk awaiting visits by reluctant users. Nice work if you can get it, but it costs an arm and a leg, for a start. While they wait for users, the music reference librarians I know are no longer sitting at the desk "reading magazines"—charitably,

---

David Lasocki is head of reference services in the William and Gayle Cook Music Library, Indiana University.
1. I explore this topic further, and especially the tempering of opinion with compassion, in "Music Reference as a Calling," *Notes* 56 ( 2000): 879–93.

they were doing their selection work—but staring at a computer screen all day long, with "interruptions" by the users. Did users employ "I'm sorry to disturb you, but . . ." as their opening gambit in the magazine-reading days? Perhaps only sarcastically. Now they get the picture: your real work is on the computer, and they are secondary. After all, *their* real work is on the computer, and they are consulting you only because (1) the much vaunted online catalog is user-unfriendly, (2) they spent two hours searching the Internet and, amazingly, didn't find what they were looking for, and (3) their friends told them that, despite the computer-glazed look on your face, you are actually a human being, and an intelligent and helpful one at that.

If "artificial intelligence" becomes as smart as real intelligence, won't reference librarians be out of a job? Not in my lifetime, I'll wager. The computerization of the planet has brought more, not fewer, questions to the reference desk. In the bad old days of the card catalog—a few ultra-conservative musicologists still wish we hadn't thrown the darn thing away—users were little inclined to approach the reference desk to see if the library owned the item they were looking for. They searched the card catalog and, if they didn't find what they wanted, tended to assume that the library didn't own it. Skill in using the catalog was taken as a given. Few users dreamed that the card catalog was user-unfriendly—which it certainly was. Now at least, users can invoke the magic computer if their search is unsuccessful. The humble approach: "I'm not very good with computers, so I was wondering if you could help me find X." Or the blustering approach: "I'm astonished that your library, which everyone says is supposed to be one of the best music libraries in the country, doesn't have Y; I've tried all the possible keyword searches. . . ."[2]

Once you attract your users to the reference desk, you can try to teach them something—that is, one thing per visit, or they tend to forget the lesson—about keyword searching, or truncation, or uniform titles, or whatever it is they need to know to make their way through the exigencies of *AACR2* and *LCSH*. Yes, I'm talking about bibliographic instruction, if that term hasn't been phased out in favor of something more trendy. I dream about our music school having enough space in its curriculum, and me having enough time in my work day, to teach all the students in the school how to use the library so well that they wouldn't need to come to the reference desk. I dream about offering mini-classes to users other than music students and having them actually show up.

---

2. This was a real "question." The user was looking for a score of Beethoven's *Archduke Trio,* and she fell into two common library traps: knowing only a nickname for a work, and employing the singular of a generic term when the uniform titles and subject headings of library catalogs are geared to the plural. What price catalog reform?

Actually, I dream about holding classes and having all the students in any class show up, rather than skip it as a soft option ("Oh, it's only library instruction" or "Oh, it's only Lasocki again—we heard everything *he* has to say in our last class"). Differently put, I dream about the day when I will be classed as the teacher that I am, rather than as a "reference librarian." I do keep dreaming, even though my reality is worlds away and receding. Everyone pays lip service to the need for bibliographic instruction, but the task is mammoth. Meanwhile, we do a great deal of instruction, one-on-one, at the reference desk.

How else has the electronic revolution changed music reference? If you know what you are doing, it has sped up research. (If you don't know what you are doing, it has left you doing things like standing at a terminal typing "a=mozart" with two fingers, then spending two hours wading through the resultant five thousand entries.) Thanks to keyword searching, Boolean operators, and truncation symbols, databases yield certain kinds of information that printed sources cannot. Databases are also faster to use and more current than printed sources. Through MLA-L and other distribution lists, we can get rapid help from our ever-generous colleagues. Because of OCLC and its kin, interlibrary loan has become much faster and more visible—and the recent introduction of downloadable files of dissertations augers well. Web sites, so colorful and magnetic to today's users, especially the generation brought up on Sega and Nintendo, also hold the promise of an unprecedented currency of information.

But of course speed and even currency aren't everything. The most important thing I have tried to teach the students in my music bibliography class is how to evaluate reference sources. We simply cannot accept reference "information" at face value but must endlessly ask ourselves about its purpose, authority, source, intended audience, context, and accuracy. My students are rightly horrified at the slipshod and brainless way some reference books are put together—and I won't even get into Web sites. The students are also amazed that we are still lacking some obvious reference books, the latest example that came up in the class this week being a thematic index of the works of Rossini. In 1992, Deborah Campana gave a talk at the MLA annual convention in which she reported on an informal survey she had conducted among music reference librarians about new reference sources, or enhancements to old ones, that they would like to have appear.[3] The main items on the wish list— better forms of song indexing, retrospective periodical indexing, a real

3. "Music Reference in the Nineties: Resources." I am grateful to Dr. Campana for sending me a copy of her unpublished talk.

music-in-print, better biographical information on contemporary figures, an update to Heyer, an index to *The New Grove,* and so on—were identical to a similar list collected by Ann Basart a decade earlier.[4] Eight years on, we are getting an update to Heyer,[5] and the *International Index to Music Periodicals* has made a start at retrospective periodical indexing, but the fundamental point stands: we are lacking some basic reference sources we would dearly like to have. And, as you can bet my students now know, just as important as the subject matter is the quality. Campana went on to reiterate Walter Gerboth's point from 1982: "We need reference works that are first-rate, and a major factor in first-rate is that they be user-oriented."[6] She concluded that music librarians "need to be involved with the design phase of major reference resources"—that is, to express our opinions, voice our concerns, describe our experiences, look for better models, and review and evaluate products.

I couldn't agree more. I fervently believe that it is our mission, as music librarians of whatever stripe, to give advice to publishers and Web-site compilers about the content and usability of reference sources. MLA's own guidelines for music reference works,[7] already six years old, need to be disseminated widely and continually. In this era of databases, we especially need better-designed databases, with more subject terms. Beyond trying to influence others, we need to keep creating our own reference sources—at the very least, to replace our old vertical files and in-house card files of songs and local music events. The Gaylord Necrology File is an example of what a committed music librarian can achieve on the Web.[8] Ann Basart did not merely report the lack of music reference sources; she started her own publishing company, Fallen Leaf Press, to help fill the gaps. The new Heyer is of course partly due to her work behind the scenes. Even I, who love to philosophize, am putting my money where my mouth is: in 1998, in response to one of my most frequent types of reference question, I began constructing *Musicians' Dates,* a Web-based file of birth and death dates with source references.[9] Perhaps I shall even get to the letter Z before I retire.

    4. *Cum notis variorum,* no. 66 (October 1982): 3–5; no. 67 (November 1982): 30–32; no. 69 (January–February 1983): 13–14.
    5. George R. Hill and Norris L. Stephens, *Collected Editions, Historical Series & Sets & Monuments of Music: A Bibliography* (Berkeley, Calif.: Fallen Leaf Press, 1997). The index has been promised on CD-ROM.
    6. *Cum notis variorum,* no. 67 (November 1982): 32.
    7. David Hunter et al., "Music Library Association Guidelines for the Preparation of Music Reference Works," *Notes* 50 (1994): 1329–38.
    8. Nathan Eakin, comp., "Gaylord Music Library Necrology File," http://library.wustl.edu/Units/Music/necro.
    9. The URL is http://www.music.indiana.edu/musicref/datestop.htm.

Technology has placed increasing demands on all reference librarians: to keep up with the hardware at the rapid pace of the computer industry and to learn how to use an increasing number of online reference sources, in addition to dealing with more questions and more instruction sessions. But technology is only one of many pressures faced by reference service. Fifteen years ago, Bill Miller already noted six different problem areas: (1) the success of reference service was leading to increasing demand; (2) new activities for reference librarians were continually being added; (3) reference librarians, having decreasing time for professional growth, were falling behind in it; (4) the workload for reference librarians was growing; (5) the success and increasing workload were not being compensated; and (6) reference librarians were eventually burning out, and the quality of their work declining.[10] Since Miller's article, and partly in response to it, various attempts at reference reform have been made. Yet, assessing those reforms recently, David A. Tyckoson found them wanting.[11] Expert systems have not found acceptance. E-mail and chat-lines provide far worse service than the telephone. Tiered reference service (professionals, paraprofessionals, student assistants) and, to some extent, team staffing are failing because the people in the lower tiers are unskilled at the reference interview, and because users hate both waiting and being referred to other staff. Making appointments with reference librarians works well only for advance questions from users who don't mind waiting and being referred. I should add that what is potentially the best reform of all—giving enough money to provide an adequate number of reference librarians—has of course not been tried, because no one has thought it worth spending the money on. Increasing the reference staff by employing catalogers, collection development librarians, and administrators on the reference desk is hardly a long-term solution, simply because it takes those people away from cataloging, collection development, and administration, which are always with us.

Music reference requires a deep knowledge of music as well as education and training in librarianship. Are we going to continue to attract qualified people to the profession? I must say that I am probably more concerned about this question than any other I have posed. The music-librarianship program at Indiana University is one of the few left in the country, and whereas a dozen years ago we could choose among a dozen well-qualified applicants, today we are lucky to find three or four per

10. Bill Miller, "What's Wrong with Reference: Coping with Success and Failure at the Reference Desk," *American Libraries* 15 (1984): 303–6, 321–22.

11. David A. Tyckoson, "What's Right with Reference: The Failures and Successes of Reference Reform," *American Libraries* 30 (1999): 57–63. I am grateful to Ralph Papakhian for bringing this article to my attention.

year who actually come. Balanced against that, I am encouraged that our music librarianship students now want to do internships on the reference desk, where once they tended to work solely in cataloging.

Where does that leave us? I believe that, in this digital age, we need strong music reference service more than ever—at the reference desk, in the instruction room, or beating a path to a publisher's door. We need more and better reference sources, whether they are formatted as books, databases, Web sites, or some newly invented medium of the future. Music reference librarians need time for training and development in that challenging but endlessly fascinating dance with users, computers, and reference sources. We need to persuade our colleagues, cohorts, supervisors, deans, directors, presidents, trustees, and taxpayers that music reference is a vital function that deserves their funding. Above all, we need to encourage qualified people to enter the profession and join the dance. Will you, won't you? Will you, won't you? Won't you join the dance?

# REFERENCE SOURCES

## By John E. Druesedow

———————————————— ◇ ————————————————

### THE PAST FIFTY YEARS: A VARIETY OF LANDMARKS

There was a time, half a century ago, when each new monthly issue of *The Music Index*[1] was eagerly sought and carefully inspected by researchers for new pieces of bibliographic information gleaned from such periodicals as the new *American Musicological Society Journal* (*Music Index*'s terminology for the *Journal of the American Musicological Society*), *Etude* (now long gone), the *Musical Quarterly* (then with its familiar yellow cover), *Notes* (of course), and the *Hospital Music Newsletter* (a trimestral publication now nearly forgotten; the annual subscription fee was $1.00); there were eighty-one periodicals listed in the 1949 annual cumulation (presently about four hundred titles are indexed).

In 1949, the fifth edition of *Grove's Dictionary of Music and Musicians* had yet to appear; *Baker's Biographical Dictionary of Musicians* was in its fourth edition; the fifth edition of *The International Cyclopedia of Music and Musicians* was brand new; and the first fascicles of *Die Musik in Geschichte und Gegenwart* (*MGG*) were being published.[2] It took two decades to complete *MGG* in its basic fourteen volumes; another decade passed before the two supplemental volumes were issued, then seven more years for the appearance of the final volume, the index—seventeen volumes in all, 1949–86. General editor Friedrich Blume provided an account of those first twenty years in an article in *Notes,* in which he described some of the vicissitudes of such a lexicographical undertaking in wartime and postwar Germany as well as the very high ideals that were in fact realized.[3] Harold Samuel, the editor of *Notes* at that time, inserted an enthusiastic footnote, which began:

> One of the most significant musicological undertakings of our time, if not of all time, is undoubtedly *MGG*. Nearly twenty years ago, as we studied the first fascicles of Volume I and were amazed at the scope of the undertaking,

---

John E. Druesedow is music librarian at Duke University.

1. *The Music Index* (Detroit: Information Service, 1949–87; Harmonie Park Press, 1987–). Until 1964, *Music Index* was subtitled "The Key to Current Music Periodical Literature."
2. Eric Blom, ed., *Grove's Dictionary of Music and Musicians*, 9 vols. (London: Macmillan, 1954; suppl. vol., 1961); Theodore Baker, *Baker's Biographical Dictionary of Musicians*, 4th ed. (New York: G. Schirmer, 1940); Oscar Thompson, ed., *The International Cyclopedia of Music and Musicians*, 5th ed., ed. Nicolas Slonimsky (New York: Dodd, Mead, 1949); Friedrich Blume, ed., *Die Musik in Geschichte und Gegenwart: Allgemeine Enzyklopädie der Musik*, 17 vols. (Kassel: Bärenreiter, 1949–86).
3. Friedrich Blume, "*Die Musik in Geschichte und Gegenwart:* A Postlude," *Notes* 24 (1967): 217–44.

who among us did not have doubts about its ever being completed? But it has been completed and is probably the most widely used work on the library's and scholar's reference shelf. How could we possibly get along without it![4]

Five years after the beginning of *The Music Index* and *MGG*, the fifth edition of *Grove's Dictionary of Music and Musicians* was issued in nine volumes—all at once.[5] A paperback reprint of this edition, which included the supplementary volume (1961) appeared in 1970. This was to remain the standard music encyclopedia for the English-speaking world for over a quarter century, even though it did not reach the high standard set by *MGG*. Vincent Duckles, in the first edition of his *Music Reference and Research Materials*, made this comment in the annotation for the *Grove's* entry:

> Although the 5th ed. was completely reset, expanded, and brought up to date, it falls short of *MGG* as a tool for scholarship; however, it holds an undisputed place as the major music reference work in English.[6]

The balance of esteem between *MGG* and *Grove's* shifted when *The New Grove Dictionary of Music and Musicians,* greatly expanded in both physical size and geographical coverage, burst upon the scene on St. Cecilia's Day, 22 November 1980.[7] In a *Notes* review, the reference staff of the New York Public Library's Music Division collectively opined that "if the appearance of *The New Grove* looks like a star of the first magnitude to the musical world, it is surely a supernova to the music library one."[8] Some wondered if *New Grove* could (or should) be considered "Grove 6." Most intoned "New Grove," simply because it was so new.

It was new in physical size and ethnic coverage and also new in the sense that, under the general editorship of Stanley Sadie, it spawned a host of *New Grove* family members, such as *The New Grove Dictionary of Musical Instruments* (1984), *The New Grove Dictionary of American Music* (1986), *The New Grove Dictionary of Jazz* (1988), *The New Grove Dictionary of Opera* (1992), and *The New Grove Dictionary of Women Composers* (1994),[9] as well as a series on composers. It was also one of many "new" music ref-

---

4. Ibid., 217.
5. See n. 2.
6. Vincent Duckles, comp., *Music Reference and Research Materials: An Annotated Bibliography* (New York: Free Press of Glencoe, 1964), 8.
7. Stanley Sadie, ed., *The New Grove Dictionary of Music and Musicians*, 20 vols. (London: Macmillan, 1980).
8. *Notes* 38 (1981): 55.
9. Stanley Sadie, ed., *The New Grove Dictionary of Musical Instruments*, 3 vols. (New York: Macmillan, 1984); Wiley H. Hitchcock and Stanley Sadie, eds., *The New Grove Dictionary of American Music*, 4 vols. (London: Macmillan, 1986); Barry Kernfeld, ed., *The New Grove Dictionary of Jazz*, 2 vols. (London: Macmillan, 1988); Stanley Sadie, ed., *The New Grove Dictionary of Opera*, 4 vols. (London: Macmillan, 1992); Julie Anne Sadie and Rhian Samuel, eds., *The New Grove Dictionary of Women Composers* (London: Macmillan, 1994; American ed. publ. as *The Norton/Grove Dictionary of Women Composers* [New York: W. W. Norton, 1994]).

erence works from other publishers, for example, *The New Oxford Companion to Music* (1983), *The New Harvard Dictionary of Music* (1986), and *The New Country Music Encyclopedia* (1993).[10]

Two "Harvards" had preceded *The New Harvard:* Willi Apel's *Harvard Dictionary of Music* (1944), followed after twenty-five years by the revised and enlarged edition (1969).[11] By the time *The Music Index* and *MGG* appeared in 1949, Harvard occupied a secure niche as the most useful one-volume music dictionary in English, at least for United States readers. It contained a wide variety of term definitions as well as authoritative historical essays, but no biographical entries. A complementary resource, *The Harvard Biographical Dictionary of Music,* edited by Don M. Randel (also the editor of *New Harvard*), appeared in 1996. In 1999, Randel's *The Harvard Concise Dictionary of Music and Musicians,* a distillation of *The New Harvard* and *The Harvard Biographical,* was published, building on over half a century of "Harvard" prominence in the one-volume category.[12]

In 1967, two years before the revision of the *Harvard Dictionary,* a remarkable new index covering not only journals but also books and even parts of books was launched: *RILM Abstracts of Music Literature,* published under the auspices of the International Musicological Society, the International Association of Music Libraries, and the American Council of Learned Societies.[13] "RILM," standing for "Répertoire international de littérature musicale," is one of four major music reference sources whose titles begin with "Répertoire international" and are known generally by acronyms; the others are *RISM* (*Répertoire international des sources musicales;* 1960–), *RIPM* (*Répertoire international de la presse musicale: A Retrospective Index Series;* 1988–), and *RIdIM* (*Répertoire international d'iconographie musicale;* 1975–). The prime mover behind *RILM* and *RIdIM* was the late Barry S. Brook, well known also for compiling the major source on thematic catalogs, *Thematic Catalogues in Music: An Annotated Bibliography* (1972, rev. 1997).[14]

10. Denis Arnold, ed., *The New Oxford Companion to Music,* 2 vols. (Oxford: Oxford University Press, 1983); Don Michael Randel, ed., *The New Harvard Dictionary of Music* (Cambridge: Belknap Press of Harvard University Press, 1986); Tad Richards and Melvin B. Shestack, *The New Country Music Encyclopedia* (New York: Simon & Schuster, 1993).
    11. Willi Apel, *Harvard Dictionary of Music* (Cambridge: Harvard University Press, 1944); 2d ed. (Cambridge: Belknap Press of Harvard University Press, 1969).
    12. Don Michael Randel, ed., *The Harvard Biographical Dictionary of Music* (Cambridge: Belknap Press of Harvard University Press, 1996); idem, *The Harvard Concise Dictionary of Music and Musicians* (Cambridge: Belknap Press of Harvard University Press, 1999).
    13. *Répertoire international de littérature musicale/RILM Abstracts of Music Literature* (New York: International RILM Center, 1967–).
    14. Barry S. Brook, *Thematic Catalogues in Music: An Annotated Bibliography,* RILM Retrospectives, no. 1 (Hillsdale, N.Y.: Pendragon Press, 1972); Barry S. Brook and Richard Viano, *Thematic Catalogues in Music: An Annotated Bibliography,* 2d ed., Annotated Reference Tools in Music, no. 5 (Stuyvesant, N.Y.: Pendragon Press, 1997).

The twenty-volume format of *The New Grove,* making it the largest of the music reference tools in English, was indicative of a general expansion of the cultural base of music reference resources in the last quarter of the twentieth century. This was due in part to the expansion (some would say "dissolution") of the traditional musicological canon with its well-known emphasis on European (or perhaps at least "Europeanized") art music.

Scholarly interest in ethnic music had been evident since around the turn of the twentieth century through the work of Erich von Hornbostel, Curt Sachs, Frances Densmore, and many others, but nearly the whole century passed before such a comprehensive series as *The Garland Encyclopedia of World Music* (1998–) was undertaken.[15] Similarly, for a long time popular music had its aficionados, but only recently was this general interest supported by commensurate publications—for example, *The Encyclopedia of Popular Music,* which went through three progressively larger editions in the 1990s.[16] Nat Shapiro's and Bruce Pollock's definitive bibliography of popular songs, *Popular Music, 1920–1979: A Revised Cumulation,* appeared in 1985.[17] Patricia Havlice's *Popular Song Index* (1975)[18] remained the most useful guide for popular song anthologies. World popular music was covered admirably in *World Music: The Rough Guide* (2d ed., 1999).[19] Several *Rough Guides* now cover more delimited aspects of popular music (e.g., reggae, rock, and jazz) in greater detail, all with emphasis on recordings.[20]

Increased interest in gender studies has been reflected in a number of bibliographical and biographical sources on women's music, including *Women in Music: An Encyclopedic Biobibliography,* by Donald L. Hixon and Don A. Hennessee (2d ed., 1993), and the *International Encyclopedia of Women Composers,* by Aaron I. Cohen (2d ed., 1987).[21] Access to resources in African American music was vastly enhanced by *A Bibliography of Black*

15. *The Garland Encyclopedia of World Music* (New York: Garland Publishing, 1998–); 10 vols. projected.
16. Colin Larkin, ed., *The Guinness Encyclopedia of Popular Music,* 4 vols. (Enfield, Middlesex: Guinness Publishing, 1992); Colin Larkin, ed., *The Guinness Encyclopedia of Popular Music,* 2d ed., 6 vols. (Enfield, Middlesex: Guinness Publishing, 1995); Colin Larkin, comp. and ed., *The Encyclopedia of Popular Music,* 3d ed., 8 vols. (London: MUZE UK, 1998).
17. Nat Shapiro and Bruce Pollock, eds., *Popular Music, 1920–1979: A Revised Cumulation,* 3 vols. (Detroit: Gale Research, 1985).
18. Patricia Pate Havlice, *Popular Song Index* (Metuchen, N.J.: Scarecrow Press, 1975); 1st suppl. (1978); 2d suppl. (1984); 3d suppl. (1989).
19. Simon Broughton, *World Music: The Rough Guide,* 2d ed. (London: Rough Guides, 1999).
20. *Reggae: The Rough Guide* (London: Rough Guides, 1997); *Rock: The Rough Guide,* 2d. ed (London: Rough Guides, 1999); *Jazz: The Rough Guide* (London: Rough Guides, 1995). Two other musical Rough Guide titles are *Classical Music: The Rough Guide,* 2d ed. (London: Rough Guides, 1998) and *Opera: The Rough Guide,* 2d ed. (London: Rough Guides, 1999).
21. Donald L. Hixon and Don A. Hennessee, *Women in Music: An Encyclopedic Biobibliography,* 2d ed., 2 vols. (Metuchen, N.J.: Scarecrow Press, 1993); Aaron I. Cohen, *International Encyclopedia of Women Composers,* 2d ed. (New York: Books & Music, 1987).

*Music* (1981–84), a four-volume publication edited by Dominique-René De Lerma, and Eileen Southern's *Biographical Dictionary of Afro-American and African Musicians* (1982). The Center for Black Music Research sponsored the publication in 1999 of the *International Dictionary of Black Composers*, which included 186 extended biographies.[22] There was also an increase during the last quarter century in the sheer number of reference titles, particularly in bio-bibliography or composer series. Reference resources on music of the United States fared very well after the Bicentennial, with *Resources of American Music History* (1981), *The Literature of American Music* (1977), *Bibliographical Handbook of American Music* (1987), *Periodical Literature on American Music, 1620–1920: A Classified Bibliography with Annotations* (1988), *Early American Music: A Research and Information Guide* (1990), and *American Sacred Imprints, 1698–1810: A Bibliography* (1990),[23] all in addition to the aforementioned *New Grove Dictionary of American Music.*[24]

An increasing number of *Gesamtausgaben* and national monuments were described in the three editions of Heyer's *Historical Sets, Collected Editions, and Monuments of Music: A Guide to Their Contents* (1957, 1969, 1980),[25] which was succeeded by Hill and Stephens in the similarly titled bibliography, *Collected Editions, Historical Series & Sets & Monuments of Music.*[26] Other keys to the contents of these editions (indispensable for many music libraries) were the various thematic catalogs for J. S. Bach, Beethoven, Berlioz, Billings, Brahms, Handel, Mozart, Joseph Haydn, Schubert, Richard Strauss, and Vivaldi, among many others.

---

22. Dominique-René De Lerma, *Bibliography of Black Music*, 4 vols., The Greenwood Encyclopedia of Black Music (Westport, Conn.: Greenwood Press, 1981–84); Eileen Southern, *Biographical Dictionary of Afro-American and African Musicians*, The Greenwood Encyclopedia of Black Music (Westport, Conn.: Greenwood Press, 1982); Samuel A. Floyd Jr., ed., *International Dictionary of Black Composers*, 2 vols. (Chicago: Fitzroy Dearborn, 1999).

23. D. W. Krummel, Jean Geil, Doris J. Dyen, and Deane L. Root, eds., *Resources of American Music History: A Directory of Source Materials from Colonial Times to World War II* (Urbana: University of Illinois Press, 1987); David Horn, *The Literature of American Music in Books and Folk Music Collections: A Fully Annotated Bibliography* (Metuchen, N.J.: Scarecrow Press, 1977), supplemented by David Horn with Richard Jackson, *The Literature of American Music in Books and Folk Music Collections: A Fully Annotated Bibliography, Supplement 1* (Metuchen, N.J.: Scarecrow Press, 1988), Guy A. Marco, *Literature of American Music III, 1983–1992* (Lanham, Md.: Scarecrow Press, 1996), and Guy A. Marco, *Checklist of Writings on American Music, 1640–1992* (Lanham, Md.: Scarecrow Press, 1996); D. W. Krummel, *Bibliographical Handbook of American Music* (Urbana: University of Illinois Press, 1987); Thomas E. Warner, *Periodical Literature on American Music, 1620–1920: A Classified Bibliography with Annotations*, Bibliographies in American Music, no. 12 (Warren, Mich.: Harmonie Park Press, 1988); James R. Heintze, *Early American Music: A Research and Information Guide*, Research and Information Guides, no. 13 (New York: Garland Publishing, 1990); Allen Perdue Britton, Irving Lowens, and Richard Crawford, *American Sacred Imprints, 1698–1820: A Bibliography* (Worcester, Mass.: American Antiquarian Society, 1990).

24. See n. 9.

25. Anna Harriet Heyer, *Historical Sets, Collected Editions, and Monuments of Music: A Guide to Their Contents*, 3d ed., 2 vols. (Chicago: American Library Association, 1980).

26. George R. Hill and Norris L. Stephens, *Collected Editions, Historical Series & Sets & Monuments of Music: A Bibliography*, Fallen Leaf Reference Books in Music, no. 14 (Berkeley, Calif.: Fallen Leaf Press, 1997).

In the late 1990s, hymnological research received a great boost through the publication of Nicholas Temperley's *Hymn Tune Index: A Census of English-Language Hymn Tunes in Printed Sources from 1535 to 1820*, and the *Hymntune Index and Related Hymn Materials*, compiled by D. DeWitt Wasson. Earlier standard reference tools in this area, particularly Katherine Diehl's *Hymns and Tunes: An Index* and Leonard Ellinwood's *Dictionary of American Hymnology*, belong to an earlier generation of indexing technology.[27]

This general proliferation of resources is progressively mirrored in the five editions of *Music Reference and Research Materials: An Annotated Bibliography* (1964, 1967, 1974, 1988, 1997),[28] known to many as "Duckles," after the first compiler and editor, Vincent H. Duckles (1913–1985). The first edition covered 1,155 citations in 331 pages, including the index; the latest swelled to over 3,800 citations in 812 pages, about a three-fold increase in content altogether.

## THE PRESENT

Chapter 12 in the latest edition of Duckles covers "Electronic Information Resources" and includes a variety of bibliographic utilities (OCLC and RLIN), databases, Web sites, and the like—forty citations in all.[29] There is no doubt that such resources require markedly increasing attention on the part of music reference specialists. This is not a new situation, but it was slow in arriving. The sciences and social sciences were highly visible in the world of electronic resources well before the humanities.

One of the most important of the present-day bibliographic resources is the online service of the Online Computer Library Center, Inc., located in Dublin, Ohio, near Columbus. Its history dates from 1967, when a group of Ohio colleges and universities formed a consortium—known then as the Ohio College Library Center, or OCLC (as it is known universally now)—to share resources electronically. Online links for shared cataloging were inaugurated in 1971. Today, OCLC is, according to its "What is OCLC?" Web page, "a nonprofit, membership, library computer

27. Nicholas Temperley, *The Hymn Tune Index: A Census of English-Language Hymn Tunes in Printed Sources from 1535 to 1820*, 4 vols. (Oxford: Oxford University Press, 1998); D. DeWitt Wasson, comp., *Hymntune Index and Related Hymn Materials* (Lanham, Md.: Scarecrow Press, 1998); Katharine S. Diehl, *Hymns and Tunes: An Index* (Metuchen, N.J.: Scarecrow Press, 1966); Leonard Ellinwood, ed., *Dictionary of American Hymnology*, 179 microfilm reels (New York: University Music Editions, 1984).

28. Vincent Duckles, comp., *Music Reference and Research Materials: An Annotated Bibliography* (New York: Free Press of Glencoe, 1964); ibid., 2d ed. (New York: Free Press, 1967); ibid., 3d ed. (New York: Free Press, 1974); Vincent H. Duckles and Michael A. Keller, *Music Reference and Research Materials: An Annotated Bibliography*, 4th ed. (New York: Schirmer Books, 1988); ibid., 4th ed. rev. (New York: Schirmer Books, 1994); Vincent H. Duckles and Ida Reed, *Music Reference and Research Materials: An Annotated Bibliography*, 5th ed. (New York: Schirmer Books, 1997).

29. Duckles and Reed, 5th ed., 613–22.

service and research organization dedicated to the public purposes of furthering access to the world's information and reducing information costs."[30] Music scores and recordings presently account for more than two million of its over forty million bibliographic records, or over 5 percent. Online access to *RILM Abstracts of Music Literature* through OCLC's FirstSearch has been available since 1996; *RILM*'s database is now approaching 250,000 records. OCLC's WorldCat, also available through FirstSearch, offers unparalleled access to its entire database of bibliographic records. *Dissertation Abstracts Online* is also offered through FirstSearch.

The Research Libraries Information Network, Inc., known as RLIN and sponsored by the Research Libraries Group (RLG), offers an alternative to OCLC through its services and access to over thirty million bibliographic records. Its sophisticated online bibliographic service, somewhat similar to OCLC's WorldCat, is called Eureka.

OCLC and RLIN are described as bibliographic utilities, from which comprehensive services (cataloging and authority files, interlibrary loan, and reference databases, for example) are available. Together with other resources accessible through the World Wide Web, they comprise an immense and bewilderingly diverse array of resources that is continually expanding. Viewing the Web through any of several powerful search engines seems remotely similar to viewing the expanding universe through the lens of the Hubble telescope.

Resources available through the Web are challenging the primacy of printed materials available on the shelves of our libraries. Certain kinds of reference information can be identified much more quickly and efficiently through the Web, and, furthermore, certain kinds of reference information are now available *only* through the Web. Experienced researchers may be cognizant of the limitations of the Web in terms of the authority, reliability, and completeness of the information provided at some sites, while students may not be so discriminating,[31] even as resources for evaluating Web sites grow in numbers and sophistication.[32]

Digitization and transmission techniques have been improved to the point that there is little reason beyond the most esoteric to consult the original if its image in full color is available through the Web.[33] Digital or

30. http://www.oclc.org/oclc/menu/whatis.htm.

31. See Richard C. Rockwell, "The World Wide Web as a Resource for Scholars and Students," *American Council of Learned Societies Newsletter* 4, no. 4 (February 1997), 9–10, 21; also available via the Web at http://www.acls.org/n44rock.htm.

32. See, for example, Indiana University's "Guide to Research: Evaluating World Wide Web Resources" at http://www.indiana.edu/˜libugls/Instruction/Guide/self_guide6.html. The Web search service Yahoo, in conjunction with ZDNet, offers an online site for classical music: http://www3.zdnet.com/yil/content/roundups/ classical_music.html.

33. Two good examples are Duke University's Digital Scriptorium at http://scriptorium.lib.duke.edu/scriptorium and its Historic American Sheet Music Project at http://scriptorium.lib.duke.edu/sheetmusic.

"virtual" libraries are certainly more than a dream at this point. But they have not yet supplanted the print collections of most libraries for research purposes.

What *is* the present state of electronic sources? Most are gravitating toward the Web if they are not already there. The limitations of the stand-alone CD-ROM in terms of access and distribution, not to speak of revision and updates, are obvious to those accustomed to online research. There are thousands of homepages related to music—perhaps tens of thousands—some compiled by enthusiastic amateurs, and others under the sponsorship of, for example, music departments, music libraries, national archives, or well-known scholars. Many homepages are themselves bristling with links to further resources, so that exploration along a particular cyber trail could continue indefinitely. There are, to be sure, many redundancies, and an extensive search in a defined subject area can lead one again and again to the same home page. This déjà vu syndrome, familiar to online researchers, may try the patience of some, but on the other hand may indicate sites of significance, somewhat like the repeated references in citation indexes such as the *Arts & Humanities Citation Index.*

### FUTURE CONSIDERATIONS

The past is only partly (and often inaccurately) known, the present is fleeting and occasionally difficult to interpret, and the future is unknown but sometimes predictable. Despite these uncertainties, it is useful to consider the future in the short run for tentative planning purposes. If we should predict correctly and have our temporal telescope pointed in the right direction, we may be advantageously situated, eventually. Here are some areas of concern to keep under surveillance:

*Comprehensive online resources.* The *New Grove Dictionary of Opera* recently became available in an online format. This is the first significant encyclopedia of music with an online version, and its searching and revision capabilities will be closely scrutinized. The second edition of *The New Grove* will become available in 2000 in both print and online formats, according to the publisher. For some researchers, the ability to search for names and terms in various combinations across the entire text, plus the continuous revision of the text and bibliographies, will no doubt render the related print publication obsolete. Continuous revision will on the one hand be a great boon to efficiency for those who use online reference sources but may be frustrating for those seeking "the last word" for their scholarly work. When, indeed, should they cease checking for the latest data or interpretation before committing an original article or book to some state of permanency? Will anything, under these circumstances, ever be "finished?" The date stamp will become an essential element of a bibliographic citation, no doubt.

*Access through classification and cataloging of online resources.* As Web sites proliferate, some sort of general classification or hierarchical system of organization will become imperative. (The efficiency of random access is inversely proportional to the magnitude of the collective resources.) Web materials will continue to be sifted, selected, and sorted out in various ways, through imbedded metadata construction and by various search engines and portals, with Yahoo so far being one of the more sophisticated portals in presenting an organized report with collective hierarchical groupings in response to keywords submitted by the user. It will probably be up to libraries to provide necessary enhancements for efficient access to selected materials.

*Linked resources.* Newer software for digitizing and compressing audio and video (such as MP3) facilitates the linking of reference and other texts to media resources. Thus, an article in an online encyclopedia could well link a sound source with a music example and allow the user to bypass a trip to a playback station. This kind of efficiency and easy access to sound in greater or lesser "bites" will heavily influence the content of reference sources and will further influence techniques for research as well as teaching and learning. Similarly, the full text of bibliographical source materials could in some cases be provided along with online versions of scholarly publications. This would allow an "on-the-spot" comparison of the text and footnote sources.

*Universal access.* With more widespread access to both the text about and the sound of musics of various kinds plotted along the ethnic/pop/art music spectrum, it is conceivable that Western art music may enjoy something of a renaissance in the most unexpected places, well off the highways and byways of Western or Westernized culture. In this case, the need to explicate this music within cultures far outside those of Europe and North America may develop. New kinds of reference works and new finding aids will be needed, and interdisciplinary, cross-cultural expertise plus technical savvy will become premium qualifications for those who will write and compile them.

Music in general seems to be undergoing a swiftly moving process of "microculturalization" with shifting boundaries and enclaves within enclaves, and with lifestyle, age, gender, geography, history, and ethnicity all factored into this rich mix. Most of the music reference resources able to thrive in this cultural climate will doubtlessly be online.

# USER EDUCATION

## By Leslie Troutman

———————————◇———————————

A late-twentieth-century reference interview in the music library of my local institution of higher learning:

> *Erstwhile Researcher:* (*obviously frustrated*) I need information for this paper I have to do on Schubert's Trout Quintet.
> *Reference Librarian:* Okay, what have you done so far?
> *ER:* Well, I looked in the computer and I found some good stuff, but it's not enough. My teacher told me I have to have three books and three articles.
> *RL:* Did you check the online catalog or use one of the periodical indexes?
> *ER:* I'm not sure . . . I did do a Hotbot search on the Web. . . .
> *RL:* (*to herself*) Oh boy . . . one more time . . . (*to the Erstwhile Researcher*) You need to use the online catalog to find books . . .

Many public-service librarians have had this conversation of late in one form or another. The interchange illustrates an ever-increasing need for strong programs in user education and information literacy in our schools and libraries. In most cases, the problem is not finding information—we are inundated with it both in print and electronically—rather, it is teaching our users how to discover, evaluate, and use *appropriate* information.

Whether we call it user education, library-use instruction, or bibliographic instruction, the goal is the same: to teach our users to be effective, efficient, and independent researchers. Librarians have, of course, been teaching their clientele how to use the library for a very long time. Yet, as a formal discipline, with its own body of literature and designated practitioners, bibliographic instruction is a relatively recent phenomenon, dating from the early 1960s. The emphasis has been placed primarily, although not exclusively, on instruction within the academic community. A collective act of self-defense by public-service librarians, the development of bibliographic instruction roughly parallels the "information explosion" of the second half of this century. This flood of informa-

Leslie Troutman is music user services coordinator at the University of Illinois at Urbana-Champaign.

tion, in large part created by advances in technology, affects every aspect of our work as librarians. As Evan Farber notes,

> In examining library use instruction over the past thirty years, it is easy enough to point to those factors that have changed; all, or certainly almost all, of the changes relate to computer technology.[1]

Thirty-five years ago, our intrepid Reference Librarian would have shown our Erstwhile Researcher the card catalog, *Music Index,* and possibly the area where the Schubert biographies were shelved. Today the list of possible resources is quite a bit longer: the online catalog, the card catalog (still used in many libraries; Erstwhile Researcher: "What's a card catalog?"), three or four printed and electronic periodical indexes, and, yes, the Internet (that Hotbot search really *did* turn up some useful information).

What contributions have music librarians made to the practice of bibliographic instruction? In October 1986, a conference on music bibliography was held at Northwestern University in Evanston, Illinois. The conference report, published in 1993, contains no fewer than seven papers devoted to library-instruction topics. In one of those papers, Beth Christensen outlines the projects and presentations undertaken by association members in the years 1978–86.[2] She notes that while bibliographic instruction as a formal discipline within librarianship began in the early 1960s, it was not until the formation of the Midwest Chapter Bibliographic Instruction Committee in 1978 that music librarians began to concentrate their efforts in this area. Instructing the user in the ways of the music library had long been a concern; now that concern had a focus.

Christensen's article details other significant landmarks, among them the *Directory of Bibliographic Instruction Programs in the Midwest;*[3] the day-long preconference on public services and bibliographic instruction that preceded the 1982 MLA national meeting; the creation of the MLA Bibliographic Instruction Subcommittee in 1983; and the publication in *Notes* of "Bibliographic Competencies for Music Students at an Undergraduate Level."[4]

1. Evan Farber, "Plus ça change . . . ," *Library Trends* 44 (1995): 430.
2. Beth Christensen, "Music Library Association Projects on Bibliographic Instruction," in *Foundations in Music Bibliography,* ed. Richard D. Green (New York: Haworth Press, 1993), 153–56; published simultaneously in *Music Reference Services Quarterly* 2 (1993): 153–56.
3. Music Library Association Midwest Chapter, Bibliographic Instruction Committee, comp., *A Directory of Bibliographic Instruction Programs in the Midwest* (n.p.: Music Library Association Midwest Chapter, 1982).
4. Music Library Association Midwest Chapter, Bibliographic Instruction Committee, comp., "Bibliographic Competencies for Music Students at an Undergraduate Level," *Notes* 40 (1984): 529–32.

As the first list of library skills specifically directed at music students, this article is particularly significant. Divided into two parts dealing with writings about music and the musical artifacts themselves, the article offers both a skills-based and a tools-based approach. The authors identify thirteen different skills (for example, "locate journal articles in indexes and abstracts") and suggest various standard reference tools appropriate to the skill (in this case, *The Music Index, RILM Abstracts,* and so forth). One of the goals for the list of competencies is to "foster critical thinking and independent library use among music students."[5]

In 1996, slightly more than a decade after the publication of "Bibliographic Competencies," the Midwest Chapter Bibliographic Instruction Committee—by then renamed the Public Services Committee—planted the seeds for another important article, one that greatly expands upon the notion of critical thinking addressed in the earlier article. The authors of "Information Literacy for Undergraduate Music Students: A Conceptual Framework"[6] incorporate concepts from the fields of learning theory and cognitive development that were becoming prevalent in library education at that time. Setting aside specific sources and particular skills, the authors describe four broad concepts to be used as a basis for bibliographic instruction in the field of music: (1) how information is identified and defined by scholars, (2) how information sources are accessed intellectually by users, (3) how information sources are organized physically within libraries, and (4) how information sources are structured.

Through these articles, music librarians attempted to codify the skills and tools necessary for teaching clientele to think critically and act independently. Even as we did so, the rapid development of electronic information technologies greatly increased the complexity of the library environment. We began moving from librarian-mediated searching of databases and indexes to end-user searching. And although we knew we needed to teach concepts and not specific tools, we felt compelled to teach mechanical skills first before we could even begin to think about teaching concepts. Our handouts and instruction sessions were given over to explaining when to enter information where on the screen and what to push afterward. This problem was exacerbated by weaknesses in our first- and even second-generation online systems, which were inferior to the card catalog, particularly for locating music materials. Consequently, when preparing to teach, we found ourselves spending a significant part of our time trying to puzzle out how to work around the deficiencies of our new electronic "time saver."

5. Ibid., 530.
6. Amanda Maple, Beth Christensen, and Kathleen A. Abromeit, "Information Literacy for Undergraduate Music Students: A Conceptual Framework," *Notes* 52 (1996): 744–53.

Librarians, possibly even more than the teaching faculty, quickly became aware of the need to integrate user education into the music curriculum, particularly in light of the changes in technology and the flood of newly available information. We recognized that many of the students being graduated were not library or information literate. These same changes also had a significant impact on the teaching faculty. Pressed for time as they tried to incorporate more information into the same number of class sessions, an older generation of faculty members often found it difficult to make time for the librarian or for adequate library instruction. Moreover, these same faculty members were pressed as they struggled to maintain their own research skills in the face of fundamental changes in their work environment. The next decade will see a new generation of classroom instructors who were educated in our brave new technological environment. Will they more readily seek out the librarian as a partner in the educational process?

In the current educational milieu, it is vital that the librarian be flexible and creative in offering an assortment of opportunities for instruction. We have all had occasion to work with our clientele one-on-one at the reference desk. As class sizes increase and lines at the reference desk become longer, however, it is not always possible to provide satisfactory instruction in this setting. An ideal for many of us is working with teaching faculty to integrate instruction into the classroom or studio. This type of instruction is frequently presented in one or two class sessions of a basic survey course. Semester-long courses, focusing on information literacy in music and taught by music librarians or by a faculty-member/librarian team, occur less often, particularly at the undergraduate level. Integrated instruction is tailored specifically to the audience, since the needs of students in a piano studio are quite different from those in an undergraduate music-history course or a graduate course in choral literature.

Computer-assisted instruction (CAI) arose alongside our first online catalogs. As the personal computer became commonplace in the library, we longed to take advantage of this new tool for library-instruction purposes. Besides, a substantial portion of our clientele seemed fascinated by the technology. Unfortunately, the rapid pace of technological change meant that the CAI program we spent weeks creating was obsolete the following year—the software antiquated and the hardware out the door.

Not all attempts at CAI in the music library became technological dust. Two related articles in *Foundations in Music Bibliography* address this form of library instruction in use at Indiana University in the late 1980s. Michael Fling and Kathryn Talalay report on two programs at the IU Music Library used to teach students about music uniform titles and basic reference tools.[7] Like all initial attempts at computer-assisted instruction, use of these programs was limited to the computers they ran on. With the development of the Internet and the creation of programs and software tools that allow for shared programs and systems, it has been possible to move beyond the stand-alone computer. Currently, the Indiana University uniform titles program is available on the Music Library's Web site[8] and can be used by anyone to instruct music students in this very difficult concept.

Printed bibliographies, handouts, and guides are found in every library. Often devoted to a specific topic or directed at a particular segment of a library's clientele, these print materials have been migrating to the Web in recent years. The MLA Bibliographic Instruction Subcommittee, recognizing that a guide prepared for one library could be adapted for another, created the "Directory of Music User Guides for Libraries." Begun in 1996 and periodically updated, the Web-based directory has been one of the subcommittee's major initiatives. Its stated purpose "is to bring together in one place descriptions of user guides that have been developed for music collections with information on obtaining copies of the guides."[9] The guides are organized into eight subject areas: Bibliographies and Pathfinders, CD-ROM and Electronic Sources, Course Syllabi and Outlines for Library User Education, Finding Aids for Scores and Recordings, General Guides to Music Collections, Newsletters and Acquisitions Lists, Online Catalog Guides, and Miscellaneous Guides. Many are available immediately via a hypertext link, and contact information for the guides' producers is provided for those not available on the Web.

In addition to its music user-guides project, the Bibliographic Instruction Subcommittee sponsored the opening plenary session at the 1990 national meeting in Tucson. Two of the five presentations were related to technology (instruction methods for CD-ROM products and a report on one of the Indiana University CAI programs mentioned above). The remaining presentations dealt with the "one-shot" approach to instruction; the teaching of a formal, semester-long course in music bibliography; and a report on the bibliographic-instruction survey con-

---

7. Robert Michael Fling, "Music Bibliographic Instruction on Microcomputers: Part I," in *Foundations in Music Bibliography*, 157–63 (also in *Music Reference Services Quarterly* 2 [1993]: 157–63); Kathryn Talalay, "Music Bibliographic Instruction on Microcomputers: Part II," in *Foundations in Music Bibliography*, 165–81 (also in *Music Reference Services Quarterly* 2 [1993]: 165–81).

8. David E. Fenske, Michael Fling, Brenda Nelson-Strauss, and Shirlene Ward, "Making the Most of the Music Library: Using Uniform Titles," http://www.music.indiana.edu/collections/uniform/uniform.html.

9. Music Library Association, Reference and Public Services Committee, Bibliographic Instruction Subcommittee, comp., "Directory of Music User Guides for Libraries," http://www.library.yale.edu/~segglstn/mugdir.

ducted by the subcommittee. In recent years, diverse topics have been considered at the subcommittee's open meetings: the development of an information literacy course for undergraduates; library instruction for foreign speakers of English; and the creation of an interactive Web site that directs patrons to music research materials.

The Bibliographic Instruction Subcommittee serves as one locus for user-education discussion within the Music Library Association. Music librarians, however, discuss library instruction and information literacy topics in a variety of forums. On the national level, the Education Committee sponsored an "Ask MLA" session entitled "New Approaches to Bibliographic Instruction" at the 1995 annual meeting. Instruction topics were also part of the "Ask MLA" session on "Managing Technological Change" in Seattle in 1996. In sponsoring "When You Can't Be in Ten Places at Once: Writing Effective Computer Procedurals for Your Patrons" at that same meeting, the Public Libraries Committee demonstrated that patron-education issues are not only an academic concern. Finally, the association's subject-specific groups have also contributed to the discussion through presentations such as "World Music, Multiculturalism, and Bibliographic Instruction" offered by the World Music Roundtable in 1995.

User education is also a key concern at the chapter level, where the variety of topics is as great as at the national level. Within the last decade, chapters have held sessions on bibliographic instruction for the music undergraduate (Southeast and Chesapeake Chapters' joint meeting, October 1991); the evaluation of bibliographic instruction (New England and New York Chapters' joint meeting, October 1995); bibliographic instruction and the Internet (Chesapeake Chapter, October 1996); and a review of instruction programs within the chapter (Midwest Chapter, October 1996).

Over the past ten years, MLA members have learned to speak their minds via MLA-L, the Music Library Association electronic-mail distribution list. This electronic forum has changed much about professional communication for the association's members. Surprisingly, little discussion of library instruction topics has occurred. A search of the MLA-L archives uncovered several discussions concerning bibliographic instruction and music uniform titles as well as one rather heated discussion pitting reference folk ("My users don't look for it that way") against catalogers ("Teach them how to use the catalog"). While there were a number of postings on the topic of information literacy, only two involved exchanges between members of the association; the remainder were announcements of conferences and presentations from outside the organization. Could it be that user-education issues are so institution specific that electronic discussion is not useful? Our conference presentations at both the national and chapter levels would belie this assumption. Or, are we all so busy doing bibliographic instruction that we have no time to discuss it electronically with our colleagues?

The phrases "bibliographic instruction," "user education," "library instruction," and "information literacy" were not absent in MLA-L postings. They occurred numerous times in announcements for presentations, conferences, and online-training opportunities. However, there was yet another source of postings for these terms: job announcements. A rough count of postings from early 1990 through the middle of 1999 yielded over fifty position descriptions that included at least one of these terms. Clearly, instruction is a big part of our jobs and those who write the position descriptions recognize its importance. Are music librarians really devoting as much time to user education as these position descriptions indicate?

In twenty-five years, when a future editor of *Notes* asks a group of authors to pause and ponder the profession's recent past, what will have captured my counterpart's attention? While my crystal ball returns only the most nebulous of answers, I predict that the following four issues will form the heart of user-education discussions in the coming decades: the design and evaluation of instruction opportunities formed in direct response to the needs of our user communities; a commitment to continuing education for the librarian; the innovative and creative use of technology; and library instruction for diverse populations, whether physically in the library or in distance-learning situations.

In order to understand the instruction needs of our users, we must listen closely and then plan and evaluate our efforts carefully. Developing a close working relationship with faculty members and classroom instructors is not a new issue but rather an issue that will become more critical as time passes. With ever-increasing information sources easily at hand, instruction will need to be made relevant to the immediate needs of the user. Moreover, we must be flexible enough to provide opportunities for instruction at the point of need through both CAI and more traditional methods such as handouts and guides. At the same time, we have the responsibility to help construct comprehensive and coherent user-education programs that strive to produce information-literate library users. Both faculty members and administrators—in the library and the institution—should understand the music librarian's value as a teacher in this context.

In order to earn the confidence of faculty and administrators, we must continually sharpen our own instruction skills. While it may appear a daunting task, we need to discover and absorb new technologies and teaching skills without losing those still valuable to us. Since our library administrators apparently value user education as a part of our jobs, we must help them understand that resources need to be devoted to continuing education for the instruction librarian. Library administrators should offer—and librarians should take—the opportunity for staff training and continuing education in order to improve their own teaching skills.

The World Wide Web is one example of this type of continuing education need. It offers wonderful instruction opportunities for library users in all types of libraries. In upcoming decades, instruction librarians will need to be well versed in preparing Web sites and creating electronic assignments and learning opportunities. Distributed instruction across the Web will make it easier to reach large classes with minimal effort on the part of the instruction librarian—after she learns how to write the Web page. The Web will allow the public librarian to offer appealing interactive instruction to populations only marginally served before. Many institutions go to great lengths to create technology initiatives for education. The instruction librarian should try to participate in these.

Technology will continue to have a profound effect on the way learning happens in our educational institutions. Not only will it shape the way courses are designed and delivered, but it will also affect the way users access information and the skills they require in the workplace and beyond. The physical walls of the library are breaking down, especially as distance learning increases in popularity. Moreover, our user populations are becoming increasingly diverse in age, language, and cultural heritage. We must design intuitive systems to instruct those who never or only rarely enter the library as well as those for whom traditional methods are less than effective.

Once a foundling left under the music library reference desk, user education is maturing into a gangling young adult, ever eager to learn and become independent. The technological revolution of recent decades requires that this youth mature quickly. Music librarianship has always attracted those who have sought the challenge of administering multifaceted collections and the demand of providing comprehensive access to diverse materials. We pride ourselves on the depth of our subject knowledge and our ability to answer the tough question. In the same spirit, music librarians have taken the first steps in developing and delivering effective library-instruction programs. As we continue to grow and improve as library educators, we will keep in mind the ultimate goal: creating independent and literate music library users.

# MUSIC PUBLISHING

## By George Sturm

———————————— ◇ ————————————

Music Publishing. The *art* of bringing a *musical product* to a *public.*
What could be more obvious? But in order really to understand music
publishing, one must be clear on the meaning of these three simple
terms.

My choice of the first term is almost playful. Is publishing an art or just
a business like any other? It probably has elements of both. It involves,
first of all, a deep understanding of and respect for music and its makers,
composers, and performers. Ideally, it should also suggest the sustaining
of several simultaneous relationships, each as unique as the personality
of the composer who freely chooses to entrust his or her career to the
care of a publisher (or more often, a particular personality on a publisher's staff). These relationships must be based on mutual trust, with
both parties reserving the right to speak their minds, knowing that ultimate decisions are the composer's prerogative. (The composer can always terminate a relationship and switch to another publisher.) In that
sense, publishing is as personal and discreet as state diplomacy. Once the
composition has been created, the business dimension arises with a sizable agenda that includes expertise in engraving, copying, and computer-
setting; editing, marketing, and distributing; such administrative skills as
contracts, royalties, and copyrights; and the related enterprises that keep
the music industry afloat.

The musical product, of course, is the commodity being marketed
and ranges widely from hymns, anthems, and other church music, to
methods and other educational music, to jazz, pop, blues, rap, rock, folk,
show, and ethnic, to that many-splendored blip on the charts known as
concert music. While recent trends in the writing, publishing, and distributing of printed music seem to show a vague coming-together of
disparate elements, compartmentalization is still more the rule than the
exception: people do their own thing and have little connection with or
interest in areas outside their own competence.

Which leaves the final and, in some ways, the most important of the
three terms: the public. Which public? It takes no deductive brilliance to
observe that there are many publics making up the market for printed

---

George Sturm is executive director of Music Associates of America.

music. It is incumbent on each publisher to determine what products are best suited to the market with which it is most familiar.

And here is where the history of music publishing should be considered. When it all began in eighteenth-century Europe, some enterprising music lovers put their tastes and talents to the task of satisfying a mounting musical appetite among a steadily growing army of middle-class amateurs. Everybody sang or played, and the experience of teaming up with others was enormous fun. Composers were more than happy to oblige by writing music that was within the grasp of these amateurs. Moreover, since cities were far more isolated from one another than ours are today, each urban center was more or less autonomous and self-sufficient and had its own musical amateurs (in the best sense of the word) who hungrily clamored for access to whatever the local tunesmiths were providing for their particular instrument or ensemble. Did you want to hear what a new piece sounded like? You sat down and played it, either in the original version or in one of the myriad arrangements brought out to fill popular demand. No wonder then that a profusion of *Kleinmeister* evolved to become the minions of countless parlors and salons. And on the music stands was the printed music turned out by a new breed of publishers—such as Breitkopf & Härtel, the firm that "organized the trade of music along modern business lines, keeping a large stock of printed and manuscript scores and issuing periodical catalogues remarkable for their thematic indexes."[1] Music publishing, in the modern sense, had begun.

It was the same Breitkopf & Härtel, almost two hundred years later, that was to show the way in America by opening a New York office in the 1920s, soon to be joined there by a convocation of other music publishers who foresaw the gathering storm clouds over Europe and wished to safeguard their property by having inventory and doing business in America. Now called Associated Music Publishers, this company—once owned by Muzac, subsequently by BMI, and in more recent times by G. Schirmer, Macmillan, and Music Sales—joined the core of indigenously American music publishers—including Oliver Ditson, Carl Fischer, G. Schirmer, and others—in supplying printed music to the American market in educational, popular, church, and concert music.

But how that market had changed since the halcyon days of Johann Gottlob Immanuel Breitkopf! By the middle of the twentieth century, the significance of so-called "paper sales" lay primarily in music that sold in great quantity—for example, successful piano methods, vocal scores to the great choral monuments, and so on. Income from the sale

---

1. Paul Henry Lang, *Music in Western Civilization* (New York: W. W. Norton, 1941), 724.

of vocal, chamber, and contemporary music drastically decreased as home musicmaking began to dwindle. On the other hand, publishers began enjoying revenue from the copyright itself—from performances, broadcasts, recordings, synchronizations, and diverse licensing rather than from the sale of printed editions.

On the surface, the outlook for music publishing seemed fairly bright as the twentieth century passed the halfway mark. Publishers could still afford their "travelers," sales people who toured the country in their cars, describing their new issues to music dealers and writing sizable stock orders that more than paid their way. In marking its centenary in 1961, G. Schirmer published *One Hundred Years of Music in America,* a set of essays edited by Paul Henry Lang that presented a formidable overview of most aspects of musical life by the foremost authorities, including, besides Lang himself, Nathan Broder (on the American composer), Helen M. Thompson (on the American symphony orchestra), Nicolas Slonimsky (on American concert life), Edward Downes (on critics and criticism), and others.[2] One essay in this book, however, was both prescient and ominous. Richard F. French's "The Dilemma of the Music Publishing Industry" was not only deadly accurate in its reportage on the publishing scene, past and present, but an unsettling prognostication of what the industry would be facing in the times ahead. "The industry may not die," French wrote, "but to remain alive it must first try to see the present for what it is and prepare to deal with the future. As it searches out the new, it may learn much about itself, about society, and about music."[3]

French's study was particularly significant because it viewed music through the eyes of the sociologist and dared to question concepts and institutions that had long gone—and still continue to go—unchallenged. One such idea that should be of great concern to music publishers is that people no longer have to make music themselves, now that modern media put music at the disposal of a passive society. If it is true, as French and others have suggested, that our mass media have contributed to the erosion of musical literacy and that, in fact, we have geared contemporary musical products to meet the standards of the lowest common denominator, then it is small wonder that concert music, an abstract artistic expression that makes considerable demands on its listeners, has come to attract a smaller and smaller public. How well meaning are those who

2. Paul Henry Lang, ed., *One Hundred Years of Music in America: A Centennial Publication* (New York: G. Schirmer, 1961).

3. Richard F. French, "The Dilemma of the Music Publishing Industry," in Lang, *One Hundred Years,* 173.

desperately search for the right gimmick or gadget that might pull in more young people, old people, multicultural people, et alia! How noble, and yet, how mistaken. For the fact remains that unless you succeed in educating people, from as young an age as possible, to participate in the musical experience, to become musically literate, you will perforce wind up with passive people with minimal musical standards. A dismal picture for publishers of concert music.

Let's take another look at *tempi passati*. Alfred Loewenberg's *Annals of Opera, 1597–1940* is an invaluable reference work.[4] Quite apart from the compendium of information it contains about some four thousand operas, it shows us at a glance that any opera of even moderate note, written during this vast span of time, enjoyed multiple productions, each with a cluster of performances within a decade or two of its creation. Here we read that Christoph Willibald Gluck's *Orfeo ed Euridice* (1762) had twenty-six *productions*, including one in Charleston, South Carolina, before the end of the eighteenth century. Between the 1837 premiere in Vienna of Donizetti's *Lucia di Lammermoor* and 1850, the opera was given numerous performances in each of the following cities: Madrid, Paris, Lisbon, London, Malta, Baden, Berlin, Prague, Lemberg, Ljubljana, Algiers, Corfu, Odessa, Brussels, Zante (Zakinthos, Greece), Amsterdam, Budapest, Athens, Pressburg (Bratislava), Stockholm, Geneva, Havana, St. Petersburg, Corsica, Lima (Peru), Mexico City, Copenhagen, New Orleans, Alexandria, Batavia (Jakarta), Zurich, New York, Santiago (Chile), Palma (Mallorca), Warsaw, Trinidad, Bucharest, Constantinople, Dublin, Rio de Janeiro, Buenos Aires, Christiania (Oslo), and Helsinki. Consider the economic implications for music publishers.

In a speech given at the annual meeting of the Music Publishers Association in June 1976, Hans W. Heinsheimer chillingly described the European music scene between the wars. He and his colleagues in the industry put out the works of Paul Hindemith, Ernest Bloch, Igor Stravinsky, Manuel de Falla, Ottorino Respighi, Dmitri Shostakovich, Darius Milhaud, Jacques Ibert, Arthur Honegger, Francis Poulenc, Alban Berg, Anton Webern, Erich Wolfgang Korngold, Karol Szymanowski, Belá Bartók, Zoltán Kodály, Kurt Weill, Arnold Schoenberg, Richard Strauss, Leoš Janáček, Frederick Delius, Carl Nielsen, Edward Elgar, Sergey Rakhmaninov, Jean Sibelius, and others. "They wrote for and were accepted by the general public of their day," Heinsheimer said, "and many of their works, like those of their great predecessors, have become and remain part of our musical heritage. The gap between

---

4. Alfred Loewenberg, *Annals of Opera, 1597–1940*, 3d ed. (New York: Rowman and Littlefield, 1978).

contemporary music . . . and audiences that plagues us today simply did not exist."[5] Consider the economic implication for music publishers.

Comparison is unavoidable. Clearly, the graph of the progress of yesteryear's new musical work is concentric, like a pebble thrown into the pond, reaching ever greater audiences, whereas too many of today's musical creations have their premieres, are (at best) repeated a time or two, and vanish. And yet the unsuccessful piece of music costs the publisher just as much to produce as the hit. Consider the economic implications.

But *why* this sad turn of events? Is it that composers have lost their knack? Hardly. It would, I think, be reasonable to claim that there is more of what Paul Hindemith called "the craft of musical composition" today than at any time in history, that composers have assimilated more music and mastered more disciplines—including orchestration, electronic techniques, notational and computer skills—than ever before. In fact, the cross-pollination that our musical arts have been heir to during the last decade or so has made for considerable excitement, especially when coupled with a new and more relaxed climate that has broken down hard-and-fast barriers between such previously unbridgeable forms as "serious," "entertainment," "folk/ethnic," and "theater" music, early and electronically altered music, and the various guises of tonal, polytonal, microtonal, and nontonal music.

It is not the composer's bag of tricks that publishers should look at, but the public's. What, they should be asking, does the public want from us? And if there is the sense that the public's standards are not sufficiently high, then ways must be found to raise them. How? Well, here is where a true spirit of adventure, initiative, savvy, and commitment must make itself felt.

For years, the disappearance of small, independent publishers has been lamented, not without cause. Survival has dictated a wave of acquisitions, mergers, and conglomerizations on both sides of the Atlantic as the publishing industry has, like so many other industries, been globalized. That certain properties have been lost in the wake of these mongrelizations is beyond dispute. But others may have been gained through this new largeness. A company that finds itself part of a megaconcern — a BMG, Warner, Sony, Disney—suddenly wields enormous potential political clout. Such a company might find little difficulty in bringing its values and goals to the attention of other businesses, let alone legislatures. For if there is a way to stimulate the arts, heighten public literacy, and sensitize our people to the long-term personal and national benefits of

---

5. Hans W. Heinsheimer, "Speech, MPA Meeting, June 9, 1976" (paper presented at the annual meeting of the Music Publishers Association, New York City, 9 June 1976), 6.

all the arts, then the first step must surely be through education. We should insist that arts education become a basic required component in our curricula from pre-kindergarten through college. To do this, we need professionals who are versed both in the arts and in the marketplace to show the way.

As the publishing industry enters the twenty-first century, it faces certain massive problems. One is the aging of copyrights to works that have proven popular and have represented a significant source of revenue. Many such compositions have already fallen into the public domain, thus eliminating the dimension of "rights" and legal protection, and even laying them bare to exploitation by reprint houses. Others are on the verge of having their copyrights lapse, with no new, viable replacement being found that would make up for lost income. On the other hand, composers and publishers have been granted an extension of copyright protection to authors' life plus seventy years instead of the prior fifty years. And in the case of some foreign copyrights, the GATT provisions have restored protection on certain works that had actually been in the public domain.

Another problem that has presented considerable apprehension has been the illegal photocopying of copyrighted materials. It is claimed that sizable funds are being forfeited through such reprography, but a vigorous campaign by copyright proprietors has made users aware not only of the unethical nature of such piracy, but also of the considerable financial consequences of such misdeeds by way of fines and public exposure.

The last quarter of the twentieth century has brought about some fundamental changes in the way printed music is distributed, both in the United States and abroad. In the old days, publishers depended on local dealers to promote their product. These were professionals who knew their clientele and made it their business to bring interesting new issues to the attention of respective teachers and enthusiasts. The principal task of publishers' representatives was to keep the dealers informed and give them excellent service. But dealers have gone where sales volumes lie: they sell sound equipment, guitars, other instruments and paraphernalia, and whatever sheet music that sells in significant quantity. Where does that leave publishers? Finding themselves largely without local promotional arms, music publishers at the close of the twentieth century have either established their own retail divisions—selling their product directly to end-consumers rather than relying on decreasingly effective music shops—or they have developed excellent relations with a small cadre of music distributors. Through the work of superbly skilled research staff using dependable databases, distributors save librarians and end consumers time and money by providing them, at the best available price, with printed music from publishers all over the world.

What the twenty-first century will mean to music publishers is difficult to predict. It is impossible to think that technology will not play a major part in determining what music publishers will do and how they will do it. They already use computer technology for engraving, inventory, billing, order fulfillment, royalty administration, and accounting. We are but a step away from using the Internet for the actual distribution of music. Soon we will order precisely what we need for our orchestras, choruses, and libraries through the Web and download our music from cyberspace. What will this mean for publishers? What must we do to assure the continued protection of intellectual property? What will be the position of the librarian who is committed, at the same time, to serving the interests of patrons while also working in tandem with authors, composers, and copyright proprietors?

And, of course, music publishers will be asking themselves what they should be publishing. The works of the great masters have been published and republished in up-to-date editions. We are running out of *Kleinmeister*, and besides, who will buy the lesser works of bygone centuries if and when even the printed masterworks of yesteryear have lost relevance to some degree?

My bet is on composers and musical amateurs. It may be that the former will want to write a simpler music once again, and that the latter will want to learn how to sing and play it rather than hearing someone else in some mechanical reproduction, no matter how high the fidelity. Yes, my hunch is that kids will be taught to read, sing, and play. What they then choose to do with their skills will be up to them. But you can be sure that there will be composers to provide new and satisfying music for them, and music publishers to make it available in whatever way modern technology will allow.

# SOUND RECORDINGS

BY TOM MOORE

———————————————————— ◇ ————————————————————

Sound recordings are a fundamental resource for American music libraries as they enter the twenty-first century. This represents a change
from the status quo at mid-twentieth century, when sound recordings
could be viewed as supplemental to the basic mission of the music library, which was to provide scores (viewed as the true embodiment of
the musical work) and writings about those scores (music literature).
Changes in American and world musical culture mean that the score is
increasingly viewed as a blueprint for the actual realization of the work
in sound, represented by the recording. This is a viewpoint closer to that
characteristic of other performing arts, where what matters more is the
performance: the ballet, not its notated choreography; the play on stage,
not in the playbook; or indeed, the building, not the blueprint. Thus it
may well be more important for the music library to make the recording
accessible rather than the score, even for what we think of as "classical"
music, music inheriting the tradition of the European musical canon.

These changes in our musical ethos have become evident in a number
of places. One prime example is the way in which composers and compositions are evaluated by competitions, by their peers, by the search
process leading to academic employment, and by performing ensembles.
These are all situations in which many, if not all, of the evaluators can be
expected to be musically literate, to be able to grasp the musical argument of the composer or her composition by reading the score, with or
(preferably) without the aid of a keyboard. Nevertheless, recordings of
the works being considered have come to be highly recommended or
mandatory. Composition competitions note that "wherever possible, a
tape of the work(s) should be included" (International Festival for Contemporary Music, "Musica Nova Sofia 2000"); for some, the "quality of
recordings is not critical" (Recorder 2000 Composition Competition),
"professional tape quality is not required" (Alienor Harpsichord Composition Awards); for others "the recording must be a professional-level
performance" (the Louis and Virginia Sudler International Wind Band
Composition Competition, which goes on to specify the most desirable
form of cassette tape). The Bang on a Can Festival (New York City) requests cassette tapes; scores are specifically disinvited, though DATs,

Tom Moore is assistant music librarian at the Scheide Music Library, Princeton University.

73

videos, or CDs may be submitted in lieu of cassettes. A similar situation obtains both for composers who are searching for their first academic job and for those who are being reviewed for tenure. Here, the more important criterion is the recording's release on a commercial label, perhaps roughly equivalent to a book publication in other areas.

What are the economics of commercial recordings for contemporary composers? Underwriting is key. Most recordings of contemporary music, even if offered on the market by a for-profit company, will never sell enough copies to recoup the costs involved with their production. Typically, a record company may expect to receive five dollars or so for each unit sold, from which costs associated with producing the recording must be subtracted. These include the cost of reproducing the disc itself and of reproducing the booklet, which may be of equal or higher cost. Far costlier, however, are the steps that lead to the final edited DAT or CD-R delivered by the producer to the record company. These may include union-scale pay for the musicians involved in the recording, the cost of renting the recording site (which may approach or exceed one thousand dollars a day), and the cost for the engineer who will record and edit the final product (this can range from approximately two thousand dollars to over five thousand dollars). The agreement between the record company and the supplier of the recording may involve payment of a licensing fee by the company to the supplier, and royalties paid per unit sold. This will be the case, however, only if the company expects to be able to sell the recording at a rate that will allow it to make a profit. More likely in the case of contemporary music is that the supplier of the recording will agree to pay the record company a substantial amount to offset the losses it is likely to see in making the recording available commercially. This sum can vary, but may certainly be as much as five thousand dollars, an amount from which the record company will recoup the costs of production and promotion. Thus the cost to the supplier of the recording may easily amount to ten thousand dollars or more. The sobering side of the equation is that this expenditure is required to put on the market a recording that may sell only one or two hundred copies. Doing the math shows that the cost distributed over these one hundred copies is at least one hundred dollars per copy, an order of magnitude over the retail cost, or you might consider that each retail buyer is subsidized at about 600 per cent. What is surprising, given the economics, is that there are dozens of such recordings released each year. Nevertheless, the incentives of professional recognition, both in terms of employment and visibility within the musical profession, mean that, for now, these recordings are mandatory for the contemporary composer.

The economics of recording classical music in general are better, but only somewhat. Sales figures are higher and may range typically between one thousand and ten thousand. This means that the record company may be willing and able to pay a licensing fee and royalties. Some companies eschew royalties and simply pay a one-time fee. Even at the higher end of sales, the amount of royalties paid will be an insignificant sum in the context of the income from performance fees for a successful group. Recordings are thus a means of putting the performer's work before the public, rarely a source of significant income. The visibility that recordings confer is, for performers just as for composers, essential. No performing ensemble can reasonably expect to make their case to concert presenters and to tour successfully without a series of commercial recordings.

Music libraries have been fortunate in the past in that the small part of the musical universe on which we have decided to focus our attentions has been disproportionately well served by the recording industry. Classical music may have been less remunerative to sell than popular music, but it had the less pecuniary rewards of prestige and social standing. As classical music has lost in its esteem in society in general, it has suffered both from declining sales in the recording industry and a concomitant unwillingness to continue pouring capital into a losing proposition. Although sales of recorded music have continued to climb world-wide (doubling in value in the last decade),[1] the portion of this that could be described as classical continues to fall, from around 10 percent of the market a generation ago to only 3 percent or so today in the United States. (In a market selling around a billion recordings a year, thirty million are classical.) A substantial part of the blame for this trend must be assigned to the failure of the United States to continue to support music education in its public schools, often a victim of measures intended to end increases in property taxes, with music seen as an expendable frill. The largest share of sales for recordings are made to the fifteen-to-nineteen-year-old bracket, and the numbers drop continuously with increasing age. It seems reasonable to assume that the average sixteen-year-old learns more about the Backstreet Boys from MTV than she does about Bach in her classroom.

Will the recording industry continue to supply the recordings that we want to add to our collections? In spite of the declining market for classical recordings, there have been some rewarding trends in the last few

---

1. Pekka Gronow and Ilpo Saunio, *An International History of the Recording Industry*, trans. Christopher Moseley (London: Cassell, 1998), 193.

years. Among these have been the success of recordings of early music and performances on period instruments, (paradoxically) the glut of recordings of standard repertory, and the increasing globalization of trade.

The success of early music in appealing to the musically literate with disposable income has been a major change in the configuration of the classical music scene in the last twenty years. Even in the later seventies recordings made on historically appropriate instruments were rare and limited to a small number of labels. At that date it was not difficult to find a disc that claimed to be the first recording of a particular master-work on authentic instruments. The eighties saw an increasingly large share of the market for recordings of late-eighteenth-century repertory (Mozart, Haydn, and Beethoven symphonies) go to period-instrument ensembles, though with varying reception from record critics. The nineties continued that trend into the nineteenth century, with period instruments and techniques applied to music by Mendelssohn, Berlioz, Brahms, and Wagner, and even extending to music composed in the early years of the twentieth century. At this writing, recordings of baroque music on other than period instruments are rare. The success of this record-industry niche has meant that the ensembles involved have been able to continue to explore previously unrecorded repertory in the area of early music, works previously known only to musicologists in scholarly editions (operas by Georg Phillip Telemann, oratorios by Alessandro Scarlatti, chamber music by Christian Cannabich—the list is endless).

Even ensembles devoted to later music played on the instruments of the late-twentieth-century orchestra have been more adventurous in choice of repertory, and often by reason of necessity. Recordings of the central works of the repertory (Beethoven and his Germanic successors) have signally failed in their sales, as they now must compete with almost a half-century of high fidelity—and two decades of digital—recordings. This has meant that the symphonies of Gian Francesco Malipiero, Anton Rubinstein, or almost any of the minor figures usually relegated to dis-cussions of musical nationalism, are now available for libraries.

The increasing globalization of trade has also meant that recordings from small enterprises (these represent the one-third of the market share not held by the five or six largest multinational corporations domi-nating the business) are now more easily available in the United States. At the end of the LP era in the early eighties, it may have been possible to learn about a recording made in Europe, in the Soviet bloc, or in South America or Asia, but the chances of acquiring it for the library without traveling there were slim, unless the record label was distributed in the United States. Improved communications with the advent of the Internet have meant that a library can easily order directly from the recording's country of origin. Companies distributing product in the United States do so on the expectation that the level of sales will support their cost in promoting the product. (This is the reason for the frequent frustration of the collector who sees that one of the multinationals has made a recording available in Europe, but not in the U.S., fearing that the item will not sell.) Being able to order easily overseas means that this bottleneck no longer stands in the way of acquiring important recordings for the library.

At this writing, perhaps the major unanswered question in the area of sound recordings is how the ability to distribute sound files easily over the Internet will affect the economy of the recording industry, and hence what music is recorded and distributed. In 1999, a large-scale transition towards virtual distribution of sound files over the Internet seems still quite distant for a variety of reasons, and hardly more realistic than a similar process for the written word. Libraries will continue to collect both printed books and sound recordings in a physical medium for some years yet, the hopes and dreams of some librarians notwithstanding. There are a variety of reasons for this. One of the most important is that, at least for now, the quality of sound available over the Internet is not comparable to what the listener expects from the compact disc. The time required to download a sound file, with the most recent compression algorithms, is substantially more than the file's playing time. Perhaps most important, the cost differential between the hardware required to play a compact disc or cassette and the hardware needed to receive and play sound files from the Internet is enormous.

One of the most substantial challenges to those building collections of sound recordings is the continuing change in the curriculum of music schools and departments, and in a broader sense, the changes in music consumption for the society as a whole. Throughout most of the LP era, many music collections restricted their scope to the western European canon, narrowly defined, with little interest in the erudite musical production of countries outside the central triumvirate of France, Germany, and Italy, and with even less interest in popular music, whether from the NATO bloc or elsewhere. The eighties and nineties saw a substantial evolution in the music under consideration even in the more conservative musical institutions. Jazz (though some would say, to deleterious effect) has gained a permanent place, with jazz ensembles everywhere and formal instruction in many places. As this was an area of neglect under the old dispensation, the nature of jazz as an art transmitted aurally, whether in performance or on recordings, has called for substantial collection-building in this area. Popular music, though less often the focus of instruction, has become increasingly the object of study in the academy, whether in the music school or department, or as is more frequently the case, elsewhere, whether in the context of history, language and literature, or sociology. This is also an area where the sound recording is fundamental, and the notated score secondary or nonexistent and, once more, an area neglected in earlier years. Finally the erudite and popular music of non-Western cultures (India is a good example) is increasingly of interest.

Selecting intelligently in so many areas requires continuing education on our part and the time to read broadly. The collector focusing on the Western canon is well served by a number of familiar magazines (*Gramophone, Fanfare, Diapason,* and *American Record Guide*), though it is important to bear in mind that for market reasons, many recordings of interest, even in this narrow area, may never be reviewed. More challenging is the effort to keep up with recordings we need to buy that are outside of their purview, especially recordings of contemporary music. This requires spending time finding reviews in a wide spectrum of narrowly focused periodicals, which may be aimed at jazz, early music, Australian music, and so forth. A useful source of information, unaffected by pecuniary considerations, is the electronic-mail distribution list, where aficionados can share facts, news, and opinions. The specialist in each of us needs to share, through our more general discussion lists (MLA-L and others), our meetings, and our publications, the information that will be of broader interest.

# THE ANTIQUARIAN MUSIC MARKET

## By John and Jude Lubrano

———————————————◇———————————————

Commerce in antiquarian music materials is a small but vibrant part of the "business" of the wider world of music. This commerce is conducted internationally, mostly by specialist antiquarian booksellers dealing exclusively in the subject area of music. The materials they handle include early and rare printed music and music literature, and music autographs and manuscripts. Some music antiquarians also handle music iconography in the form of prints, drawings, paintings, and vintage photographs, all with musical subjects. The traditional open shop with general antiquarian materials including a well-stocked music section is generally a thing of the past, as most open shops today no longer include music in any serious way among their subject specialties. In the same way, established dealers in new printed music and music literature who used to have significant antiquarian departments no longer handle rare materials, with one or two exceptions. "Ye Olde Musick Shoppe" with its dim, dusty corners where a musical gem or two might be lurking is also all but a thing of the past. The times they have a-changed, are a-changin', and will continue to a-change, as we hope will be made clear in this article.

As something of an aside, a distinction should be made here between dealers in truly antiquarian materials and dealers in scholarly materials (i.e., used and out-of-print music and music literature). While there is a dearth of the former, many of the larger secondhand bookshops will often carry a sizable stock of scholarly music books in addition to used music. There are, in addition, a number of dealers, both in the United States and abroad, who specialize in scholarly out-of-print music books.

The majority of today's music antiquarians conduct business not from open shops but rather from offices, either in their homes or on some commercial premise, and are usually open to visitors by appointment. They often publish catalogs of selections from their stock currently being offered for sale, describing these items in considerable bibliographical detail. Music antiquarians have comprehensive reference libraries to enable them to research and catalog their stock. They often sell a significant percentage of their stock by making individual offers to clients based upon a detailed knowledge and appreciation of a particular client's collecting interests. They may also wear a number of other hats,

John and Jude Lubrano are the owners and proprietors of J & J Lubrano, Music Antiquarians.

including those of advisor, broker, agent, and appraiser. In addition, some music antiquarians are, in fact, scholars in their own right, particularly in various aspects of music bibliography and printing and publishing history.

As music is such an "international language," most music antiquarians have an international clientele and do business with both private and institutional buyers worldwide. The international nature of the business often requires travel to visit clients, to visit colleagues, to attend auctions or scholarly conferences, and to perform appraisals. The advent of the fax machine and electronic mail have even further enhanced the internationalization of the music antiquarian's business.

A great deal of what was offered on the antiquarian market until, say, ten or fifteen years ago was sold to institutional collections. There was a good demand and a reasonably good supply, and prices were, in retrospect, relatively modest. Many of the music librarians responsible for collection development during this period were quite sympathetic to the collecting of antiquarian materials and actively advocated for funding for antiquarian acquisitions.

Much of this has, however, changed since that time. The march of technology has required libraries to use necessarily limited resources to look to the future—that is, toward computerization—rather than to the past, in the form of antiquarian collections. Funding is required not only for computer hardware but also for a vast array of software. This software, as a result of the digitization of special collections, often enables the user to view computer images of antiquarian items, thus, some would argue, reducing a library's need to acquire original source materials. In much the same way, the availability of fine facsimiles of music manuscripts, rare printed music, and rare music literature has also affected the market for antiquarian materials. (It could also be argued, however, that the availability of reproductions of original source materials through both print and electronic media increases awareness of these materials and thus may, in fact, encourage the collecting of original sources, at least in the private sector.) The veritable explosion in book and periodical publishing has put further demands on libraries' limited resources. All of this has resulted, in some cases, in a significant reduction in the number of institutions acquiring antiquarian materials, and also in the budgets of those institutions that continue to collect.

Despite the decrease in the institutional purchase of antiquarian materials, however, the market continues to thrive. In some instances, institutions have established special funds for antiquarian purchases, either through their own financial systems or through financial assistance from outside the institution, such as funding supplied by private sources.

These institutions have thus managed to continue to acquire both significant single items and important collections. Acquisitions will often be made because of their relevance to the existing holdings of the institution or because of their pertinence to the current research activities of their faculty. Purchases are also being made by institutions in the anticipation of scholarly need or purely because of the specific appeal (such as rarity or historical significance) of a particular antiquarian item or items.

Individual collectors have remained an important part of the market. If anything, the influence and buying activity of this group have increased considerably over the past few years, in part balancing the decline in institutional buying during the period. A large percentage of private collectors in the past tended to be either academics or those involved in music professionally in some capacity, with interests that often lent themselves readily to the collecting of antiquarian materials. This situation has changed somewhat, and there now are more and more private collectors whose professional lives are unrelated to music. The nonmusical professional status of these new collectors presents a new set of challenges to the music antiquarian.

Many private collectors tend to be quite focused, often collecting only in the specific areas pertaining to their individual interests. The increased activity in all areas of collecting has brought a considerable number of new collectors to the antiquarian music market. It sometimes comes as quite a surprise to many new to this pursuit that it is actually possible for them to acquire both rare editions of music and music literature as well as autograph letters and music manuscripts of major composers. This is due, in part, to the common misconception that these types of materials are the province of only the very wealthy or the most prestigious academic institutions. The pinnacle of collecting would be, to many, the acquisition of an autograph music manuscript by an important composer, in much the same way that the acquisition of a painting by an important artist would be to the fine-art collector.

Values of antiquarian music materials have increased consistently within this ten-to-fifteen-year period, although at a rate considered modest compared to that of some other subject areas of the rare-book and manuscript field. If recent auction results are any indication, however—and they generally are—rare music materials are now being more strongly sought after in the international marketplace. This is in part due to the increasing interest in rare books and manuscripts in general, as well as to the perception by collectors both private and institutional that music has been undervalued for some time.

When one compares the market value of first editions of important musical works by major composers to similar material in fields such as literature, science, or history, music has, over the period in question, lagged rather far behind. Similarly, rare music treatises have, until recently, been comparatively inexpensive. While early scientific treatises have been selling for tens (and in some cases hundreds) of thousands of dollars, musical works of the same period and comparable rarity have gone largely unnoticed (gather ye Zarlinos while ye may . . .).

The collecting of autograph music manuscripts and letters has had a strong following during this period, and the number of collectors for these—both private and institutional—is growing. Values have risen steadily. There is an increasing understanding that, in order to fully appreciate a composer's creative process, one needs to examine all stages of a work's evolution. This evolutionary process is often exemplified by a chronological progression through working sketches, drafts, the final manuscript, the fair copy of the manuscript used by the printer for the preparation of the first edition (often containing revisions), the corrected publisher's proofs of the first edition, the first published edition with the composer's corrections, and so on—all stages in the evolution of a work.

The two most significant factors influencing the music antiquarian today are auctions and the Internet. The former has influenced the market since the earliest days of music collecting but, in recent times, has begun to play an ever more important role in the marketplace. The latter (which is, of course, a totally new phenomenon) is only just beginning to influence the antiquarian world.

Traditionally, those wishing to dispose of antiquarian materials had the option of either selling their materials directly to a specialist dealer, who would pay them a percentage of whatever the dealer considered the potential resale value of those materials, or of consigning the materials for sale to an auction house. In the past, materials sold at auction were most often purchased by dealers for stock, to be offered later either privately or through catalogs to their own clientele. Very few collectors were aware of the auction scene, and much material was sold in large groupings in more of a wholesale setting. In recent years, however, the auction houses have encouraged more of a retail environment by heavily promoting sales directly to both private and institutional collectors. This has resulted in prices fetched at auction that in many cases represent the full retail values of material rather than the wholesale values of the past.

The music antiquarian's role within the changing auction scene is now more often one of consultant and agent acting on behalf of one or more clients than that of direct purchaser. As agent, the antiquarian is in continual contact with a potential client—from the moment the antiquarian receives the proofs of an upcoming auction catalog to the time of the actual physical inspection of the item in the auction rooms—and receives a percentage commission based upon the sale of the item being offered should the commission bid be successful.

Because of the increasingly retail nature of the auction scene and the publicity accorded major auctions (both pre- and post-sale), values fetched at auction have significantly influenced the antiquarian world. One result of the growing auction activity and associated publicity has been to allow an increasing number of people to become aware of the possibilities of antiquarian music collecting. A specialized music auction catalog often contains a diverse range of materials covering several hundred years of music history. These catalogs are commercially available and are distributed throughout the world to potential purchasers, either by subscription or on an individual basis.

Several aspects of antiquarian commerce on the Internet must be considered, each influencing the trade in its own way. There are a number of managed databases which one can search for music material by author, title, subject matter, and so forth. These databases are international and are comprised of items that represent the stocks of many antiquarian dealers, some of whom carry music. Most of the titles found, however, will be of a scholarly rather than antiquarian nature.

Some music antiquarians have their own Web sites where antiquarian materials are listed with full descriptions, much the same as one would find in their catalogs. The Web has allowed antiquarian music dealers to reach a certain number of collectors and potential collectors internationally, people with whom they would otherwise not have had the opportunity to make contact. Several of the auction houses have recently instigated plans for conducting Internet auctions in which music will feature. Up until now, little of real antiquarian interest has been offered in Internet auctions. The imminent entry of the more prestigious auction houses into the Internet world will, we imagine, dramatically affect this situation.

Supply has always been a controversial matter in the world of antiquarian music materials. It has been argued and reargued that the supply of antiquarian music simply cannot continue, and that in the not-too-distant future, there will be no more material left to buy or to sell. This has proven to be false over and over again, and it could, in fact, be stated that the materials being offered today are more numerous and just as interesting as what was offered ten or fifteen years ago. It must be remembered that, while many items have gone into institutional collections never to be resold, just as many items have gone into private collections, often reappearing on the market at a later date.

Institutions may also deaccession items from their collections from time to time, particularly those deemed not to be relevant to their existing holdings. In some cases, an institutional library may decide to dispose of rare material because of an item's considerable monetary value on the antiquarian market, then apply the funds to the purchase of material more directly related to the library's specific collecting interests or other needs.

Again, the increased publicity surrounding collectibles in general, and the often staggering prices for which some things have recently been sold, have encouraged people to reexamine anything in their possession of an antique nature. This has brought a certain amount of material "out of the closet" and into the public arena. All of these factors contribute to the continuing supply of antiquarian items to the marketplace. There is obviously a finite quantity of material, but then the notion of "antiquarian" is continually being redefined with the passage of time.

The auction factor is becoming significantly more influential in the wider marketplace as time goes on, especially with the increasing popularity and resultant impact of the Internet. Music antiquarians will, however, continue to be very important to collectors, as they provide an expertise not afforded by the impersonal nature of cyberspace. They can view the marketplace comprehensively and with a level of objectivity that allows them to assess all of its facets. They will continue to develop close working relationships with both private and institutional collectors to refine the direction of existing collections and to develop new ones. With the burgeoning of Internet commerce, there will undoubtedly be materials offered by many more people, some of whom will have neither the knowledge to describe accurately the materials they are offering for sale nor the professional expertise or experience to judge their significance or true market value. Moreover, as this Internet market develops, there will undoubtedly be a certain number of less scrupulous dealers offering materials in the marketplace, as has happened in other fields. The service of an experienced music antiquarian will be all the more valuable in this situation.

The increase in the number of private collectors that has already been seen will continue in the future. We have been experiencing a period of growing personal wealth, at least in the United States, and there are many more people who are now financially able to collect. While this situation will, in all probability, not go on indefinitely, it is expected nevertheless that the ranks of collectors with significant financial resources will continue to grow.

Many of these collectors will be interested in acquiring "high points," such as first editions of important works by major composers and significant autograph music manuscripts, as well as seminal works of music literature. There are also many areas in which there is still a considerable supply of material for which prices remain quite low. As stands to reason, much of this material dates from the later nineteenth and twentieth centuries and, somewhat surprisingly, includes the works of many major composers.

A greater degree of interdisciplinary collecting may also develop over time, as collectors with interests in related fields expand into associated music material.

As time goes on, collectors will also have the growing body of artifacts of the music of the twentieth century—both classical and nonclassical—to draw upon in addition to the artifacts of more distant eras. This will, in fact, serve to further widen the scope of the antiquarian music world in the twenty-first century. There will be collections for as long as private collectors retain their passion for collecting, for as long as institutional special collections continue to build and develop, and for as long as scholars pursue their researches and awaken interest in new dimensions of musicology.

# ARCHIVES

## By R. Wayne Shoaf

———————————————— ◇ ————————————————

In Colin Dexter's 1989 novel *The Wench is Dead,*[1] the principal character is a police detective who becomes interested in a murder case from
1859 Oxford. His interest eventually leads him to inspect the bulky original physical evidence, which has actually been preserved in police storage for nearly 140 years! The novel was dramatized and presented as an
episode of the popular PBS series *Inspector Morse.* As is true with many
adaptations, there are significant departures from the original. In the
novel, hard research and a bit of luck combine eventually to uncover the
evidence, while in the version adapted for television, a bit of luck is all
that is necessary. (In fact, a librarian who is a central character in the
novel is entirely absent in the teleplay. But then receiving credit is not
what we librarians are in it for.)

What does this have to do with music archives?

One of the problems common to all archives is public misperception.
Content and access are routinely both over- and underestimated. Few
people can really predict what an archive holds or how easy it may be to
locate and use its material. This unpredictability can result in either dis-
appointment or elation. The music archive is further mystifying because
print material is often not the principal content. Furthermore, printed
or handwritten music itself is essentially a foreign language to many potential users—intractable without translation into sound. These factors
combine to make music archives poorly understood by many.

My intent here is less to focus on what music archives are and what
they do than to look at how misunderstanding the archive's role affects
the way in which archivists undertake their mission as they move into the
twenty-first century.

Archivists have a strong curatorial role. On jury duty recently, I was
asked my occupation by the judge. I was surprised at his perplexed reac-
tion to my response of "archivist." I described an archivist as a sort of
combination museum curator and librarian. His satisfaction with my answer told me that these two professions may be better understood by the
general public, and on reflection, I realized just how much reality there
is to this combined role of storing and organizing for use.

R. Wayne Shoaf served as archivist of the Arnold Schoenberg Institute from 1987 to 1998 and is
presently team leader of Digital Resources Cataloging at the University of Southern California.
1. Colin Dexter, *The Wench is Dead* (New York: St. Martin's, 1989).

Assuring material is acquired and stored is often all that archivists can accomplish given their limited resources. Archivists' basic method of measurement—linear and cubic feet—hints at the scope of their collections. Archives can be thought of, in one way, as stores of unpublished material—primary resources—awaiting discovery and use. The sheer quantity of material stored for future use can be large, as dramatically exemplified in the closing scene of Steven Spielberg's *Raiders of the Lost Ark* in which the Ark of the Covenant is wheeled into a vast government warehouse filled with crates of multitudinous size, probably never to be found again.

But storage is just the beginning. Backlogs are anathema in archives. There is far too much stuff for it all to be described in the same detail as books are. Provenance, or knowledge about something's state prior to its deposit in an archive, is one of the underpinning tenets of archival organization and description. Since archives are the final resting place of the records—the products and, more often, the by-products of individuals and organizations generated during the course of their lives—understanding the people and institutions creating them requires an understanding of how the physical evidence of those lives was originally created and used by those entities. This material was generally not created to pass knowledge formally to others—one of the principal reasons for the creation of books—so it tends to evidence itself in a variety of ways.

It is the unpredictability of what can be important in an archive that probably causes the most confusion. For one researcher, the existence of a musical sketch may prove his thesis. For another, it might be a piece of correspondence. The evidence may be as significant as an acetate recording of a first performance or as mundane as a canceled rent check proving that a musician really lived in a particular place at a particular time. We have neither the space nor the financial resources to collect everything. In order to decide what to keep and what to discard, archivists constantly ask themselves which material could provide the most information to a potential researcher. Though the garbage and the gems are usually easy to recognize, it is more difficult to assess the potential value of most of what lies in between.

Music archivists have struggled for generations with the question of how best to make known to their potential users the contents of their archives. Libraries, on the other hand, are generally thought to contain published material—mostly print material. (Most still do. But even that is now in a state of evolution.) Cataloging and classification have successfully provided access to published material in libraries for many centuries. Books—the single largest category of published material—have many predictable characteristics, but the contents of archives do not. In the archive, cataloging and classification must be approached differently.

The finding aid has become the preferred form of access in most archives for two reasons: it offers tremendous flexibility in its content and organization, and it does not dictate the way the things it describes must be organized. Rather, the opposite is usually the case. That is, the content and organization of the material being described dictate the arrangement of the finding aid.

Codification and standardization have been slow to come to the archival world. When Melvil Dewey was teaching the principles of librarianship to a generation of Americans, most archivists had no formal archival training. Archivists tended to be subject specialists—historians mostly—who approached their charges more from the perspective of the researcher than with some well-developed methodology. They applied their own knowledge of the subject to its organization and description. This process had as many different faces as there were archivists. Early attempts at codification generally had purely local acceptance. Formal training and certification programs in the United States are a product of only the last decade or so. Archives have had fewer standards to guide them than libraries have had. On the one hand, there has been little impetus for standardization, since each archive is unique. What applies to one often has little validity for another. Only recently did this begin to change as technology injected increasing efficiency into the activity of the archive.

The archive—particularly the specialized nongovernment archive, and the music archive is usually that—seems to be the last to benefit from the technological advances of the last several decades. In the 1960s and early 1970s, computers were so expensive that they served as a solution for only large libraries and consortiums (containing mostly published materials), where standardization had created a base large enough for computers to be economical. It was not until the affordable personal computer was invented in the mid-1970s that computing technology became available to most archives. Generally, humanistic endeavors are far less valued in our society than scientific and economic endeavors. This has a direct impact on the resources available to the music archive, which does not have even the recognition value of the music library. (Although the library, too, suffers misperceptions, it is at least a "library"—something familiar to most people.)

Not surprisingly, the first use of computing technology in music archives was in the the creation of finding aids. Computers were glorified typewriters. There was no MARC format suitable for archival materials; the MARC Archival and Manuscripts Control (AMC) format was still a decade away.

In the 1980s, database programs for the personal computer proliferated. Most were nonrelational and required a heavy investment in learning. Even then, they forced compromises on the data. (Ever hear of
Y2K?) Many different operating systems competed for market dominance. None were tailored to the specific needs of the archive, much less
the music archive. Database programs were rarely compatible across plat-
forms, and many archives invested in microcomputers whose operating
systems became obsolete in as little as two years. Data already input into
such systems needed to be not only translated to a new program but also
migrated onto a different platform. From data cassette tapes and eight-
inch floppy disks to streaming back-up tapes and oxidizing CD-ROMs,
the physical format of the data was only one of the obstacles to data
longevity.

The creation of the AMC format in 1983 and its adoption by the major
bibliographic utilities paved the way to the first online databases of
archival holdings. Access to an archive's finding aids previously was limited to published catalogs or on-site visits to the archive itself, but now
any researcher in a reasonably well-equipped reference library had access to at least part of the archive's catalog from afar. But the AMC
record was still not the finding aid. Few archives had the resources to
create AMC cataloging below the collection level. Besides, to many
archivists familiar with creating finding aids as the only access, cataloging
archives in the AMC format was still like forcing a square peg into a
round hole.

The 1990s brought the Internet. For most archives, this was *the* watershed event. Suddenly even the most modest music archive could mount
its finding aids online for the world to see. As Encoded Archival
Description (EAD) has come to maturity in the last year or so,[2] the next
major step toward a truly distributed catalog has become a reality.

But easily accessible descriptive information is a double-edged sword.
As the contents of the archive have become more widely known, more
researchers are demanding access to the materials contained in the
archive. The physical material has to stand up to increasing usage. The
researcher, too, is changing. Where once only the most assiduous scholar
had the perseverance to search out, travel to, and use the elusive material found in the archive, now even the casual Web surfer places a usage
demand on the material—if only from afar, as the archivists themselves
must physically handle the materials in their archives with greater
frequency.

---

2. See Library of Congress, Network Development & MARC Standards Office, "EAD: Encoded
Archival Description Official Web-Site," http://www.loc.gov/ead/ead.html.

Preservation is more than just collecting. All traditionally published materials have a built-in preservation mechanism through the large number of copies created and distributed to individuals and libraries. Archival material generally exists in limited—if not unique—numbers, so preservation of the individual item is paramount. Preservation is expensive. It is a long-term commitment—often a gamble—considering the investment in containers, shelves, vaults, air-conditioning, and humidity-control equipment that are necessary to preserve each unique item in perpetuity.

Technology is beginning to show some promise in helping to attack the problem of preservation. Digitization of original materials is already lessening the stress of handling the physical items. If distributed description unlocks the door to access, digitization opens it.

As digital storage becomes cheaper and telecommunication becomes faster, digitization of physical items will become more economical and efficient. Today's imaging of photographic collections or digital encoding of archived recordings is only the beginning. There will be a time when digitization will be able to capture not only the audio characteristics or visual attributes of objects in three dimensions, but other physical attributes such as feel or smell.

The irony of digitization is that rapidly developing technology increases storage capacity with higher density storage, which puts more data at greater risk of damage or loss as technologies become obsolete with increasing frequency. While it is clear that digitizing for improved access is already a success, there are serious problems with relying on digital means for preservation. The issues of migration and translation as technology changes are significant. In many instances, the digital representation can never replace the analog original, so decisions must be made with regard to what should and should not be physically retained. Another issue is that of authenticity. If an analog original no longer exists, can its digital surrogate still provide the same strength of evidence? According to David Bearman and Jennifer Trant,

> Interpretation, and re-interpretation, of primary and secondary sources is the foundation of much humanistic scholarship. Construction of a convincing argument depends on an evaluation of the authenticity of source materials. Judgments about authenticity are based on assessments of the origins, completeness and internal integrity of a document. They may also draw from the consistency and coherence that exists between a particular source and others in the same context or of the same type.[3]

3. David Bearman and Jennifer Trant, "Authenticity of Digital Resources: Towards a Statement of Requirements in the Research Process," *D-Lib Magazine* (June 1998), http://www.dlib.org/dlib/june98/06bearman.html.

The greater visibility of music archives on the World Wide Web has increased potential donors' awareness of these repositories as the means for preserving their own papers. (I use "papers" in its widest definition to include anything owned or generated by an individual or institution that is potentially of archival interest.) Many music archives traditionally accepted donations of nearly anything perceived to have some lasting value. With tightened resources, however, acceptance of a gift horse is today nearly always accompanied by an examination of its dental health. Many donations will not be accepted without some level of financial support. The potential donation (or purchase) must make sense in the context of the existing collection or mission of the archive. The luxury of ever-increasing physical storage space and the hope of eventually processing everything acquired are less and less likely, so unless a collection of papers is simply too important and unique not to acquire, it had better come to the music archive with its own support mechanisms already in place and with as few strings attached as possible.

Well-crafted gift agreements are essential today. In order to protect the rights of the donor as well as those of the recipient, they must deal with intellectual rights. Archival music collections valued in the millions of dollars have become orphaned children because of disagreements as to which usages are legal and which are not. Since use gets easier as more material becomes available digitally, the issue of who owns what rights becomes even more important.

Ongoing improvements in computing technology will make the next century an exciting one for music archives, for they will be able to acquire more "virtually," catalog more, and provide greater use to a wider audience. Preservation will be an increasing concern, particularly for archives of materials from the twentieth century. Never before have we created or collected so much information on vehicles of such increasingly short life spans. The kind of historical music research to which we are accustomed will become more and more difficult, because the physical evidence—from music manuscripts written on acidic paper to compositions born at the MIDI keyboard with no physical sketches or drafts—will be more difficult to preserve and authenticate. There will be no correspondence to read because people will be communicating mostly on the telephone or via unsaved E-mail. The line between what our culture does and does not value is becoming blurred as technology makes everything equally accessible and perishable. The music archive of the twenty-first century will find collection development to be far more difficult as the physical evidence decreases and the virtual evidence increases. We will find ourselves redefining what "primary resource" really means. Either music *libraries* will take on a greater archival role as their own digital collections need to be preserved from one technological generation to the next, or the music archive itself will take a much more visible position in preservation. In other words, some of the decisions normally relegated to the music archive will become part of the music library's responsibility. This is particularly true for obtaining electronic resources; "purchasing" something today does not necessarily mean it will be on the shelf tomorrow.

I believe that technology is bringing understanding of the archive's role to a wider audience. Though it is disturbing to realize that a generation of Web surfers have a perception that if something cannot be found on the Web it does not exist, this same attitude is also pushing us to get everything onto the Web. It also introduces the danger of archivists making decisions on their own about what is and is not important, without the context of input by knowledgeable on-site users. This reduces evaluative thinking by at least one level—the on-site users—and risks the possibility that preservation decisions may be made in a vacuum.

Do people still misunderstand archives? Yes. Will misunderstandings continue? Yes. But they are already decreasing, and that translates into better access, which is the most important thing the music archive can provide.

# EDUCATION FOR MUSIC LIBRARIANSHIP

## BY JEAN MORROW

───────────────────── ◇ ─────────────────────

### TRADITIONAL TRAINING

For over two generations, members of the Music Library Association have concerned themselves with the adequate education and training of music librarians. Several articles in *Notes* and *Fontes artis musicae* and occasional statements from MLA have addressed this topic.[1] In all of this literature, the writers recognize that the basic qualifications needed for entry into the music library profession fall into three categories: general library training, music background, and knowledge of the unique issues of a music library.

In the most comprehensive discussion to date on this topic, J. Bradford Young traces the history of education for music librarianship in the United States.[2] In particular, he writes about the ongoing dichotomy that has existed for decades between the music librarian's music background and library training. Up until the early 1970s, most research library and many academic positions placed more importance on satisfying the qualifications of a music scholar than on the general skills of a librarian. Even at the time of Young's article, several prominent music librarians had never received a formal library degree. By that time, however, the library degree was considered a necessary credential for employment and most young librarians entering the profession had received their M.L.S. degree.

More often than not, music librarians have acquired their subject knowledge in a music degree program, usually before they have decided to enter the library profession. Aspiring music librarians with bachelor's degrees in music frequently undertake master's degrees in music that

---

Jean Morrow is director of libraries at the New England Conservatory of Music and teaches music librarianship at Simmons College School of Library and Information Science.

1. In 1974, MLA's Committee on Professional Education drafted a document entitled "Qualifications of a Music Librarian." Written by Linda I. Solow, Susan T. Sommer, and D. W. Krummel, chair, the statement was published in the *Journal of Education for Librarianship* 16 (1974): 53–59 and several other journals but never officially endorsed by MLA. Subsequent articles on the topic include Michael Ochs, "A Taxonomy of Qualifications for Music Librarianship: The Cognitive Domain," *Notes* 33 (1976): 27–44; Linda I. Solow, "Education for Music Librarians in the United States and Canada," *Fontes artis musicae* 26 (1979): 44–47; Don L. Roberts, "Education for Music Librarians in the United States and Canada," *Fontes artis musicae* 32 (1985): 59–62. This topic is also of concern to the International Association of Music Libraries (IAML). At its annual meetings, IAML's Commission on Education and Training undertakes a survey of training for music librarianship provided in the host country.

2. J. Bradford Young, "Education for Music Librarianship," *Notes* 40 (1984): 510–28.

provide them with advanced knowledge of music reference materials and research techniques as well as the credentials to satisfy job requirements for university positions. As Young mentions, the advent in the 1970s of joint master's degree programs in music and library science provided a new opportunity for students to integrate their music background with their library training. Previously, this type of integration had been much more difficult to obtain in unrelated, subsequent master's degree programs.

At the time of Young's article, three universities in the United States offered joint master's degrees in music and in librarianship, three universities offered an M.L.S. with a specialization in music librarianship, and four library schools offered some type of training, either a course in music librarianship or a course in music bibliography. Other library schools offered opportunities for practicums or internships in music libraries. Students who did not attend any of these schools had to learn about music librarianship on their first jobs. There they gained knowledge about the administration of a music collection, including topics of collection development, bibliographic access, shelving, preservation, equipment, and copyright issues.

The nature of the education and training required for a professional position in a music library has been determined, to a large extent, by specific job responsibilities and the size and type of collection to be served. Traditionally, positions in public libraries have emphasized public-service skills over advanced music training. Those in large research collections, on the other hand, have required a master's degree in music and occasionally a doctorate. In MLA's 1988 publication *Careers in Music Librarianship*, Laura Dankner compiled statistics from the MLA Placement Service's *Job List* covering an eleven-year period from 1976 to 1987.[3] Most of the jobs listed during these years were for administrative or cataloging positions in academic settings. Seventy-nine percent of the positions required the M.L.S.; the majority of them preferred but did not require a degree in music. Although job listings often described responsibilities usually attributed to senior-level positions, they rarely asked for more than a year or two of experience.

Present-day qualifications for entry-level positions have become more rigorous than those required in the 1970s and 1980s. The MLA Placement Service's *Job List* from August 1997 through July 1999 listed 110 jobs for professional music librarians. Over 90 percent of these required an M.L.S. and over 55 percent required at least one degree in music.

---

3. Laura Dankner, "Job Trends, 1974–1989," in *Careers in Music Librarianship*, ed. Carol Tatian (Canton, Mass.: Music Library Association, 1990), 43–56.

With the exception of a few cataloging positions that did not mention music qualifications, the remainder of the positions required, at a minimum, extensive background in music.

## CURRICULUM IN THE 1990s

Since the time that Young wrote his study of education for music librarianship, computer technology has radically transformed the workings of most libraries. It is surprising to note, therefore, that, while advertisements for music library positions continue to emphasize traditional library skills and music qualifications, only a small percentage of them mention the need for computer skills or knowledge of current technologies. Perhaps employers assume that an M.L.S. in the 1990s will guarantee the acquisition of basic competencies in library technology.

Library schools have, in fact, dramatically revised their curricula to prepare students for the demands of today's library jobs. In addition to the traditional courses in collection management and reference services, the modern library student learns to organize and retrieve electronic information and build Web sites.[4] Cataloging students now have to understand subject analysis, authority control, and technical-services management. In order to help patrons in today's complex libraries, students have to develop strong skills in both bibliographic instruction and in working with people in general. There has also been an increase in the number of students learning about the preservation of aging materials and the management of special collections and archives.

Music degree curricula have also undergone changes in the 1990s, though these have not been as extensive as curriculum changes in library schools. In response, today's aspiring music librarian needs to become knowledgeable about a wider variety of resources and collections than were available in previous decades. Today's music specialist often assists patrons working in interdisciplinary studies such as dance and art, in music of non-Western cultures, and in areas of study introduced by the "new musicology" such as gender, popular music, and music for "other purposes."

Although their academic work may be more complicated and demanding, students who wish to study music librarianship have more opportunities to do so than when Young undertook his survey of library school

---

4. Students who wish to specialize in the study of information management now have the option to undertake degrees in information science. The library schools at Drexel University, Syracuse University, and the University of Illinois at Urbana-Champaign offer an M.I.S. in addition to the M.L.S. The library school at the University of California, Berkeley, closed in 1995 and reopened as the School of Information Management and Systems. Courses in these degree programs deal not only with information retrieval and archiving documents but also with subjects that do not fall under the purview of library programs, such as interface design, online sales, and marketing.

offerings. Out of fifty-six accredited library schools, the current edition
of MLA's *Directory of Library School Offerings in Music Librarianship* lists
twelve institutions that offer double, joint, or dual master's degrees in
music and library science; three more institutions offer a concentration
in music librarianship. Thirty-six additional institutions offer either
a course in music librarianship or music library internships and
practicums in that area.[5]

Since they were first offered in the 1930s, courses in music librarianship have usually been taught by music librarians and have varied greatly
in content, depending on the emphasis of the instructor. Some instructors have focused on reference materials, others on library administration. Some have covered both topics in their courses as well as the principles of music cataloging. In the 1990s, instruction in music librarianship
deals not only with traditional reference publications but also with the
vast array of databases and resources available through the Internet.
Instruction in bibliographic access to music also includes the study of
MARC formats and the handling of music by automated systems. Classes
in music library administration educate students about the impact of
technology on library design, equipment selection and maintenance,
collection development and preservation, copyright issues, and the organization and dissemination of knowledge.

Even with the increased number of opportunities to study music librarianship in library school and the ongoing efforts of instructors to keep
coursework relevant, the most important source of education about this
topic continues to be "on the job" experience. For this critical component of our education, everyone in the profession remembers one or
more librarians who served as a mentor, teaching us the manifold workings of the music library. Whether we learned from them during a library-
school internship or on our first real jobs, our mentors have always been
and will continue to be the most important instructors available in music
librarianship.

### CONTINUING EDUCATION AND PROFESSIONAL DEVELOPMENT

More than ever before in history, today's librarian is faced with the
need to keep up with a steady stream of new information, new procedures, and new technologies. In order to meet this need, the librarian
has to seek out appropriate avenues for continuing education that can
be pursued successfully while still carrying out everyday job responsibili-

---

5. Timothy J. Cherubini, comp. and ed., *Directory of Library School Offerings in Music Librarianship*, 7th
ed. (Canton, Mass.: Music Library Association, 1998). Also available at http://www.musiclibraryassoc.
org/se_schoo9899.htm.

ties. MLA itself has identified education as one of its major areas of concern and plans to undertake several initiatives in its Plan 2001 to provide new educational opportunities for librarians working with music.

For all music librarians, MLA and its chapters have long provided the most important sources of timely information about new developments in the field. MLA's most recent annual preconference workshop, entitled "Music Librarianship and the Internet," is an excellent example of the organization's continuing efforts to educate its members and help them deal with the ongoing changes in their work environment. On a less formal basis, MLA members have utilized the MLA-L electronic-mail distribution list for several years to share information and provide professional support to each other and to nonmembers who are concerned about music library topics.

Through its Plan 2001 MLA hopes to address the needs not only of its membership but also of the large number of music library staff members not classified as professional librarians. Several current initiatives will help the organization to meet this goal. MLA's newly appointed Outreach Subcommittee is developing programs to assist the paraprofessional library worker. MLA's Publications Committee has undertaken a *Basic Manual Series* directed at librarians and staff who work in public libraries and in liberal arts collections that include music materials. Several MLA chapters have begun to organize activities geared to assisting paraprofessionals and public librarians who deal with music materials. The Mountain-Plains Chapter recently received financial support from MLA to implement a continuing-education workshop on "Music in the General Library," to be offered at state library association meetings and similar venues. Through its Public Libraries Subcommittee, the New England Chapter recently began utilizing its NEMLA-L electronic-mail distribution list as a vehicle to offer information and support to nonspecialists working in public libraries.

In addition to the resources offered by MLA and its chapters, some of our universities offer excellent opportunities for continuing education on topics in music librarianship. The annual workshop on music binding and preservation sponsored by the Eastman School of Music's Sibley Library and the music cataloging workshop given by the Indiana University Music Library are two outstanding examples.

### LONG-DISTANCE LEARNING

Perhaps the greatest potential for expanding the possibilities for education in music librarianship lies in the recent developments that have come about in long-distance learning and Web technology. Long-distance learning programs have the capacity to provide instruction on all aspects of music librarianship to a wide-ranging audience. Through Web course offerings, the music library profession could offer its know-how to those who traditionally have not had access to this information. In 1997, California State University, Los Angeles, began offering an Internet course in music librarianship through its Continuing Education Program. Designed by Nancy Weckwerth, it provides a model for what could be done through MLA.

The development of long-distance learning programs promises to enhance the curriculum at library schools as well. While on-site classroom experience offers the traditional student the advantage of personal contact with teachers and colleagues, long-distance programs will open up opportunities for M.L.S. degrees to people of diverse age groups and backgrounds who have previously lacked access to them.

## CONCLUSION

Looking ahead to the early decades of the twenty-first century, it is difficult to predict how fast and to what extent digitization will transform the nature of our library collections as well as our job descriptions. Will the basic qualifications required to manage the electronic music library differ significantly from those needed to oversee the print and audiovisual collections we have today?[6]

The urgency of this question has prompted MLA to renew its efforts to produce an official statement on the qualifications needed to be a music librarian. In winter 1999, MLA's board of directors charged its Library School Liaison Subcommittee to draft a statement on qualifications and to link it with the American Library Association Educational Policy Statements Web page. If the MLA policy statement models those of the other nine organizations currently represented on this Web page, it will include a new emphasis on personal skills as well as professional knowledge. In order to prepare library students to serve in the Information Age, these policy statements speak of personal competencies that need to be developed, such as people skills, flexibility, skills in problem solving and decision-making, ability to communicate, use of creativity and innovation, and the ability to adapt to a rapidly changing environment.

Granted, the development of such personal competencies will serve all librarians well, but MLA and the members of the music library profession must also continue to strive for the highest standards in library

---

6. A summary of skills required for the digital library of the future appeared in an article by Roy Tennant, "Skills for the New Millenium," *Library Journal* 124 (January 1999): 39. Some of these skills include knowledge of imaging technologies, optical character recognition, markup languages, metadata, indexing and database technology, interface design, programming, and Web technology.

skills, knowledge of music, and training in music librarianship. High-quality education will help us, above all, to overcome our fear of the unknown future and to carry out our responsibilities in the new millennium with skill and confidence.

# AFTERWORD

◇

> But history can also be viewed as a series of adventures—hazardous, elective exploits undertaken for the chance of great gain but with their outcome always in doubt.
>
> —Richard Ford[1]

Music librarians have accomplished much—both individually and collectively—since the founding of the Music Library Association in 1931. Our profession enters the twenty-first century on a strong footing, and we are ready to build on our record of success. If history is a reliable indicator, we will make mistakes along the way but learn from them quickly and move on. These are admittedly times of great change and uncertainty, but change and uncertainty have always been with us and in fact seem to be one of the few things we can count on. We take risks, hoping for success but never being assured of it.

What has inspired us to take these risks? What has pushed us along? What is the gain? Something must cause us to hazard failure rather than to remain secure in doing what we have always done. If not, why then do we experiment with new technologies, why do we devote years of our lives to producing new reference works, why do we sit for hours on tiresome committees? We are not pursuing wealth and fame; no one becomes a librarian for the money or the glory. Perhaps what drives us is nothing more complex than the unspoken goal of making things better—both for those around us and for those who will come later. This goal of betterment, pursued with a spirit of altruism, lies behind civilization's great achievements, and those of our own profession are no different. Is it not the goal that underlies the building of a new library, the acquisition of a composer's papers, the claim of a missing periodical issue?

The authors of the preceding essays have celebrated our accomplishments, have explained what they see lying ahead, and at times have sounded notes of caution—even about the future of our profession. As we move forward, we must continue to think inventively, to take risks—with the hope that we will succeed more often than fail—and to keep our larger goal in mind, so that our place will be secure.

---

1. Richard Ford, "In the Same Boat," *New York Times Magazine*, 6 June 1999, 106.

*   *   *

Dal centro al cerchio, e sì dal cerchio al centro
movesi l'acqua in un ritondo vaso,
secondo ch'è percossa fuori o dentro.
                                        —Dante Alighieri[2]

I end on my own cautionary note. Several essayists have touched on a trend that only indirectly affects music librarianship today but is likely to play a larger part in our future. During the course of this century, we have seen a profound change in the idea of "music," both in the academy and in society. Most of our libraries were established to support the study of Western art music (commonly known as "classical music") in college and university music departments, and this music was the focus of early collection development and reference service. Whenever other musics (usually folk and popular) were also part of the curriculum, music libraries collected sufficiently to support their study, but clearly the emphasis in most of our libraries was on classical music.

During the past few decades, the scope of musicological research has been extended to embrace many types of music that once were considered inappropriate for serious study, and traditional classical music has been reexamined through the glass of new critical theories borrowed from other disciplines. The field has broadened and diversified. Although Western art music is still central to academic music programs, the focus has become diffuse as researchers and teachers also consider jazz, rock, and other popular musics and introduce new analytical techniques into the curriculum.

In a development that is coincidental (if not causal), the role of classical music in society has evolved over the course of the century. During the early decades, attendance at the symphony and the opera was part of the weekly social ritual of the affluent and the educated, who saw the appreciation and support of music as a badge of distinction. Although the audience for classical music was never comparatively large, its enthusiasts were well placed.

During the decades since World War II, interest in classical music has slowly faded as its place in society has fallen. In the preceding pages, some essayists have attributed this fall to a decrease in funding for the arts in public schools. After all, why should people suddenly appreciate and support the arts at the age of thirty-five when they were never exposed to them in their youth? Many symphony orchestras and performing-arts organizations have tried to offset this neglect by promoting

---

2. *Paradiso* 14.1–3. From centre unto rim, from rim to centre, / In a round vase the water moves itself, / As from without 'tis struck or from within (trans. Henry Wadsworth Longfellow).

"grow your own" programs that import students from the schools into the concert hall—not to educate so much as to spark an interest in the arts that for some students might catch fire and become a life-long passion.

Members of the general public who still listen to classical music have become less tolerant of unfamiliar music. Symphony orchestras, struggling to hold on to subscribers, rarely allow programming to stray from the popular warhorses of the late-eighteenth and nineteenth centuries, and performances of post-1920 music are typically limited to the annual pops concert. Record companies and classical-music radio stations have watered down their repertory to appeal to more listeners, most of whom turn to classical music only as soothing background music[3] or as a tool for self-improvement,[4] and none of whom apparently can endure the sound of a singing human voice. We have in fact reached a point where music that was once respected by many nonmusicians—and in fact loved by some—is considered so distasteful that it is used as a repellent to discourage teenagers from loitering in parking lots and to clear vagrants out of bus terminals.[5]

As the perception of classical music changes in society, the vitality of departments and schools of music—and therefore the vitality of our own profession—feels threatened. Yes, diversity is good; the broadening of the musicological canon has energized the field. We should consider, however, the importance of instilling in others a respect—if not love— for all types of music, including the art music of the past and present. A love for this music is the reason many of us chose to become music librarians in the first place. Although we support the study of music by building collections, making them available for use, and showing others how to use them, we also have important roles to play as promoters and enthusiasts. Let us not forget the need to inspire in others the desire to enjoy a great body of music, centuries old, that has brought us enlightenment, love, joy, and consolation. Through these efforts, we can build a legacy as important as anything we might purchase, catalog, look up, or teach.

R.G.

---

3. See, for example, *Sunday with the Times* (Roswell, Ga.: Intersound/Fanfare, 1997), a four-disc recording marketed as appropriate background music for reading the Sunday *New York Times.*
4. See Don Campbell, *The Mozart Effect: Tapping the Power of Music to Heal the Body, Strengthen the Mind, and Unlock the Creative Spirit* (New York: Avon Books, 1997). By fall 1999, the theory of the "Mozart effect" had been refuted by several research psychologists. See Kenneth M. Steele, Karen E. Bass, and Melissa D. Crook, "The Mystery of the Mozart Effect: Failure to Replicate," *Psychological Science* 10 (1999): 366–70.
5. David Wallis, "Ideas & Trends: Bum-Bum-Ba-Bum; Eine Kleine Bus-Terminal-Clearing Music," *New York Times,* 8 August 1999, sec. 4.

# INDEX

◇

103

# Music Library Association
## Technical Reports Series

*Volumes available in the series:*

*The Acquisition and Cataloging of Music and Sound Recordings: A Glossary,* compiled by Suzanne E. Thorin and Carole Franklin Vidali, 1984. No. 11

*Authority Control in Music Libraries: Proceedings of the Music Library Association Preconference, March 5, 1985,* edited by Ruth Tucker, 1989. No. 16

*Careers in Music Librarianship,* compiled by Carol Tatian, 1991. No. 18

*Archival Information Processing for Sound Recordings: The Design of a Database for the Rodgers & Hammerstein Archives of Recorded Sound,* by David H. Thomas, 1992. No. 21

*Knowing the Score: Preserving Collections of Music,* compiled by Mark Roosa and Jane Gottlieb, 1994. No. 23

*World Music in Music Libraries,* edited by Carl Rahkonen, 1994. No. 24

*Cataloging Musical Moving Image Material,* edited by Lowell E. Ashley, 1996. No. 25

*Music Librarianship at the Turn of the Century,* edited by Richard Griscom, assistant editor Amanda Maple, 2000. No. 27